My Father's Daughter

Carol Caloro

I hope you enjoy my story—
Carol Caloro

BookLocker

Paperback ISBN: 978-1-64438-566-1
Hardcover ISBN: 978-1-64438-567-8

Published by BookLocker.com, Inc., St. Petersburg, Florida.

Printed on acid-free paper.

BookLocker.com, Inc.
2019

First Edition

Library of Congress Cataloging in Publication Data
Caloro, Carol
My Father's Daughter by Carol Caloro
BIOGRAPHY & AUTOBIOGRAPHY / Personal
Memoirs | FAMILY & RELATIONSHIPS / Life Stages /
Adolescence | FAMILY & RELATIONSHIPS /
Parenting / Single Parent
Library of Congress Control Number: 2019901970

To my grandchildren

Ethan, Autumn, Nicholas, Sarah and Mason

CHAPTER ONE

Mom and Dad were high school sweethearts, and ever since I was a teenager I knew my mother was pregnant when she and Dad got married. Nobody ever talked about it, but I knew the date of their anniversary and I knew the date of my birth. It wasn't rocket science. Instinctively, I knew better than to ever bring it up, because I understood that in a small rural village in the 1940s this would have been a terrible secret, a scandal, a sure source of community gossip and disdain. Where we lived, everybody knew everybody and nobody's business was private.

But Dad did like to talk about a lot of other things that happened in his earlier years. One of those things was the time he had spent in the military. It all started when he had just barely finished high school. There was a war going on at the time, and he was always very proud to have served his country. His active duty days were arguably the most memorable part of his life, and over the years he kept in touch with a few of the guys he'd met while overseas. Theirs was a bond unlike all others, and they sometimes exchanged stories and old pictures through the mail. They couldn't call each other because long distance phone calls were too expensive, so cards and letters were their only option.

***

As he approached his 18th birthday, knowing his number was coming up in the draft, he weighed his options. He presented himself to the Aviation Cadet Examining Board, part of the Army Air Corps, and was given some aptitude tests, physical exams, and all sorts of forms to fill out. He wrote in his memoirs, "Being of slight build, I did not weigh enough. Since it was lunch time, the rest of the physical was delayed. During the lunch break I loaded up on bananas. After lunch, my weight was very close, so they 'winked' and I was accepted." He was sent home to await orders to report for duty. He wrote, "Personal matters had to be handled and the most difficult was to prepare for separation from my high school sweetheart, Shirley." On August 31, 1943 he received orders to report for basic training. Because he showed suitability for pilot, navigator, and bombardier training, he was given a choice. Believing he would learn the most from navigation training, he chose to go in that direction. His education took him to North Carolina, South Carolina, and Texas, and included instruction in aerial gunnery, radio and celestial navigation, and dead reckoning. When his training was completed, he received orders qualifying him as an aerial navigator and was sworn in as a Second Lieutenant.

Circa 1944

In mid-December of 1944, Dad returned home for fifteen days. It was his first leave since entering the service, and his Christmas gift to my mother was an engagement ring. Six months later she graduated from high school and found a secretarial job with a small heating oil company in Albany. She held that job for less than two years and never worked again outside the home.

On 4/29/1946, at the age of 20, Dad was promoted to First Lieutenant. Soon after, he was released to Reserve status. He took a desk job with Gulf Oil Company in Albany, a job he would have for many years, and then on 11/16/1946 he and my mom became husband and wife. Dad's brother and

Mom's Aunt Corinne, her best friend, were their witnesses. They were married in the home of Mom's Aunt Emily, in front of a cozy fire, with a light, early snow falling softly outside. The house was a pretty little two-story brick structure, inviting and cozy. I've been in the house many times and it makes me smile to think of it. The back yard was small and full of Rose of Sharon shrubs that were always quite stunning in the summertime, and it connected to the back yard of the house where Aunt Emily's father, my great-grandfather, lived. Aunt Emily's house matched her personality and had been built for her by her young husband before she lost him to war. I never met Uncle Joe, but I have a picture of the two of them on the beach in old-fashioned bathing suits, smiling at each other while having a private conversation. She never remarried, never had children. She was sweet and funny and an active participant in church and community functions. I loved her, and one of my sisters sometimes reminds me of her, both in looks and mannerisms.

Five months after they took their vows, I made my debut. Mom was 20 and Dad was 21. I was the first grandchild on both sides of my family. My parents, my grandparents and my aunts and uncles all lived in the same small community in upstate New York, and I felt loved and happy and comfortable and safe.

In September of 1947, the Army Air Corps became the U.S. Air Force. In June of 1948 my first sister was born. We were only fourteen months apart in age and we became inseparable. Dad, although only involved in the Air Force Reserves at this point, loved the military. It suited him. He was smart, disciplined, and well-liked by both his peers and his superiors. At the end of the following year he was promoted to Captain. He was 24. In April of 1951, the month I turned four years old, and two months before Patty's third birthday, he got what I believe he always yearned for, what he was made for. He was ordered back to active duty and given a month to report to Sacramento. Instead of Dad flying to California alone, he and Mom decided to drive out together and see a little of the country. They left my sister and me with Grandma and headed out on their adventure. They wound their way through a dozen states, drove up Pike's Peak and went into Yellowstone National Park to view Old Faithful. In his memoirs, Dad recalled staying in a motel in Montana for six dollars. That price, he said, included a small kitchen and a living room. After arriving in Sacramento, Mom took up residence in a bare-bones hotel room and stayed for ten days, spending time with Dad whenever he was able. Then she took a train to Los Angeles and flew from there back to New York. This is perplexing to me because, in my experience, Mom was never a very adventurous person. I don't remember her ever striking out on her own to do anything at all. She didn't have any hobbies or interests; she didn't do anything independent of Dad. It's hard for me to imagine her traveling across the country by herself at 24-years-old. But she had to get home, so I guess she didn't have any choice.

Two months later, Dad reported to Randolph Field in San Antonio. Mom and Patty and I flew to Texas where he had rented a house for us. I don't recall the plane ride at all, or even what the plane looked like, but I do remember Patty getting air sick and making use of one of those little bags they store in the seat-back pockets for just that purpose. Leave it to a sister to remember something like that! I also don't remember much about our house in Texas, but I do remember the heat! On days when it wasn't too hot to go out, I played with a neighbor, a little Mexican boy whose mother took a 'siesta' every afternoon. He had to stop playing then and go inside. I thought siesta was a very silly word and I found it funny that an adult would take a nap every day. I also remember going to visit the Alamo. It seemed so big to me then and I was impressed by the piles of cannon balls on display. I've seen it since. It's really not so big, and the cannon balls are gone.

We spent five months in San Antonio and then Dad was sent to Topeka, Kansas. Of course, he took us with him. I was almost five by then, so my memories are a little more detailed. What I remember most is that we were there for Christmas. Patty and I got matching cowgirl outfits, complete with six-shooters, and matching baby dolls with extra clothes that hung on miniature hangers in little carboard closets. Santa also brought us a brightly painted toy roller coaster that was made out of tin. It had tiny little cars, and we loved playing with it. Between the kitchen and the living room there was a swinging door, and my sister and I would chase each other, running through the door and letting it swing closed behind us. Once, as I went through first, with Patty in hot pursuit, she stretched her arm out in front of her to catch the door before it hit her. Her hand was in just the wrong place at just the wrong time and one of her fingers got jammed. When she pulled it out it looked a little flat. Some skin was missing, and she was shrieking. Mom put ice on it right away, but the next day it was swollen and purple and sore. I felt so bad that I cried right along with her. Eventually her fingernail fell off, but Mom promised she would grow a new one.

Dad's final transfer was to Savannah, Georgia. I remember a little more about that house, especially the outside. There were snails all over the sidewalk and we stepped on as many as we could. They made a satisfying crunch. There was a glider in the yard that Patty and I liked to sit in and swing back and forth, and a clothesline that was strung between two metal supports. The supports were the shape of huge croquet wickets and we would shinny up them and hang upside down from our knees. We were once surprised and delighted that a blimp floated high above us as we hung there with the blood rushing to our heads, looking up at the sky. I also remember the terrible, blistered sunburns we both got on our backs when our mother, unaccustomed to the hot summer Georgia sun, sent us out in frilly little halter tops to play in the middle of the day. We both cried a lot that night as Mom and Dad took turns coming into our room to lay cool wet cloths across our backs. And of course, I remember the ocean. I loved the sound of the surf and the smell of the salt water. I loved going in up to my waist and jumping as a wave came rolling in, trying to stay on top of it. Mom would often take us to the beach, so there are several beach-related memories that stand out for me. First, Mom lost the small diamond out of her engagement ring while in the water there. She was frantic, but of course it was gone for good. She also lost the top of her bathing suit when a big wave came up and stole it from her. We found that to be quite giggle-worthy until she quickly halted our laughter by instructing us to hurry out of the water and bring her a towel. But the most memorable event occurred one day when Patty and I were both floating around in inner tubes. Mom was sunbathing and I was hanging out in my tube with my eyes closed, enjoying the rocking of the waves.

When I opened them, I couldn't see Patty. Then I heard some men yelling from up on the nearby fishing pier. Several of them were pointing. My sister had floated way out into deep water and she was bobbing up and down, apparently oblivious to the danger she was in. One fast-acting fisherman jumped into a small boat and retrieved her. She was fine, and not the least bit scared, but I dare say Mom learned quite a lesson that day!

In the fall of 1952, we all returned back to our sleepy little village in upstate New York. Main Street runs along the Hudson River and the rest of the village could be roughly described as four steep roads branching off of Main Street, climbing east and meeting each other at the top of the hill. Of course, there was a little more to it than that, with other small roads running north and south. We had several churches, a cemetery, a firehouse, and a school. Main Street boasted a bank, a small grocery store, a soda fountain/newsroom, a drug store, a post office, a gas/service station, a library, two bars and the Village Hall. When we were a little older, we could easily cover much of it on foot over the course of a day, even more of it if we were on our bikes. Sometimes I amused myself by imagining my parents roaming the same roads, going to the same places, even passing some of the same houses and trees when they were growing up. I found myself wishing I could go back in time and see them when they were young, spy on them in their classrooms, hear what they said to their friends, watch them walk where I was walking and do what I was doing.

Dad was once again assigned to reserve duty. I was a few weeks late for the beginning of the school year, but I started kindergarten as soon as we got home. School for me that year was held in a fire station in a neighboring community. Because I liked to sing, I recall being given a part in the Christmas pageant that our kindergarten class put on for our parents. I was to memorize an obscure verse of a popular Christmas carol and sing it as a solo after the rest of the class sang the more familiar first verse. I had practiced over and over, but still I was very nervous. Just as it became my turn I nearly ran out of the room, but I saw Mom smiling at me and I did what I was supposed to do. The following year, I would attend first grade in the basement of one of our local churches. It wouldn't be until second grade that my classes would be held in the building that was actually intended to be a school, the same school that my parents had attended from first grade right through their senior years. When I got to high school, although by then we had a new building in a different location, I actually had some of the same teachers that had taught my parents. And because I looked so much like my mother when she had been my age, one of those teachers made me laugh out loud once when she called me by my mother's name.

So, the beginning of school for me signaled the end of our traveling. They were back where they had started. Dad would continue to do two-week tours of active duty every year until the mid-1960s, but they would settle down and keep their family home. Dad wrote, "Shirley was not too pleased because I think she had come to enjoy military life."

CHAPTER TWO

In fact, my mother was often 'not too pleased', and emotionally abusive. Actually, she was spiteful, hateful, and mean. I didn't know it when I was little, but by the time we stopped traveling around and I was old enough to notice how she interacted with others, I knew something about her wasn't nice. First and most obvious was her reaction to my father's family, especially the women. Dad was not supposed to go to Grandma's house, even though it was a four-minute walk across a grassy field. He went sometimes anyhow, but not as often as he would have liked. Grandma didn't have a mean bone in her body. She did not treat Mom badly or make her feel unwelcome. She was a sweet, old-fashioned grandma – half Dutch, half German. I loved her. She would say to me much later, "Your mother was very hard to get along with." She seemed surprised when I answered, "Yes, Grandma, I know."

Grandpa was nice too, but I never felt I knew him very well. His first language was Dutch. He spoke very broken English and was often silent. I do remember climbing up on his lap sometimes and he would let me stay there as long as I wanted. And I remember his thick head of beautiful snowy-white hair. He was stricken with cancer at the age of sixty-nine and Dad walked over there every day to help turn him over in his bed. He died at home when I was fourteen. As was often the custom, his wake and funeral service were in the living room of their house. It seemed strange to see the open casket sitting on a platform in front of the big, sunny windows of that familiar living room, right next to where he always sat in his favorite chair. Mom handed me a handkerchief, but I didn't cry. It was my first experience with death and I felt more shocked than sad. I have some old postcards with handwritten messages from Grandpa to Grandma while he was in the army during World War I. He was courting her at the time and the messages are sweet, but very formal and polite. I treasure them.

Sometimes my sister and I would sneak over to Grandma's because we always knew, in exchange for a big, warm hug, we could find freshly-baked cookies in the big cookie jar on a shelf in the pantry. Grandma always wore an apron over her housedress and we often found her with flour on her apron, where she had wiped her hands as she made cookies or coffee cakes or bread dough. She was a big woman and she shuffled when she walked, as if her legs hurt, but she never complained. This was the house my dad grew up in, and Grandma still cooked on a big old cast iron stove. It had burners that she could lift off by using removable handles, revealing the fire inside the stove. In the winter, the fire was always burning because the stove doubled as a source of heat. We had to be careful not to bump into it so we wouldn't get burned. It had a high back with a shelf reaching out over the burners. The shelf was also warm and it seemed there was always some great-smelling yeast dough sitting there, covered with a clean dish towel, rising before being put into the oven for baking. What would it be when it came out of the oven? Something delicious, for sure! Have you ever smelled home-made bread baking in the oven? It's heavenly. It makes you hungry. It makes you happy. When I was a little older, Grandma would teach me how to bake brown bread in a coffee can so the slices would be round. She showed me what went into the raisin bread she made at Easter time for us to eat for breakfast with the colored eggs we had found. Her secret ingredient was a cupful of left-over mashed potatoes added to the dough which, she said, kept the bread from being too dry. And of course, kuchen. She made the best apple kuchen! It was always moist and chewy and sweet and delicious, covered with thick slices of tart apples and sprinkled with sugar and cinnamon. She would measure things like salt or cinnamon by pouring them into the palm of her hand and declaring, "That looks like a teaspoonful," then dumping them into the bowl. I still cook like that. She would make soups and stews that simmered all day and tasted as wonderful as they smelled. She made a dish called hutspot that consisted of mashed potatoes mixed with cooked onions, carrots, and greens from the garden. Often, she added crumbled bacon. I loved that! And sometimes she made oliebollen – small Dutch doughnuts with raisins inside. They were round balls with an uneven, bumpy exterior, fried to a golden brown. You could see the oil sizzling on their surface as she removed them carefully from the pan. She gave us 'coffee' to go with them. It was really a cup of warm, sweetened milk with just enough coffee to turn it slightly brown in color, but it made us feel very grown up!

Outside there was a water pump where Grandma got the water she brought in to use for cooking and drinking. I was always thirsty at Grandma's because I wanted to go out and work the pump. We had indoor plumbing and a flush toilet in our house, but Grandma did not. In the big old barn-turned-garage was a lot of random stuff, but the most fascinating thing was a 1930 Model A Ford. It had belonged to one of Grandma's brothers and it just sat there for as long as I can remember, with boxes full of who-knows-what sitting on its hood and roof. There was also a sloping cellar door on the back of the house that we could slide down and a chicken coop full of chickens and baby chicks. I loved going into the coop and grabbing a cupful of cracked corn out of the big wooden barrel so I could toss it onto the floor and watch the chickens try to beat each other to it, noisily flapping and clucking. Sometimes I was allowed to gather eggs, but that scared me a little because the chickens didn't like it when you took their eggs. The eggs provided a large part of daily meals when my dad was growing up, and as a result he hated eggs as an adult. Of course, they also ate the chickens, but I never wanted to hear about that.

Grandma had a huge garden and both she and Grandpa worked it all spring and summer. They grew lots of food, but I was always more impressed with the peonies. Huge, heavy pink blooms that hid the rest of the garden from the house. And inside she grew African violets. They were all over the window sills in the living room. All colors and varieties. It seemed to me that none of them ever died or stopped blooming. I remember Grandma had a sweet old cocker spaniel with runny eyes who liked to follow us around outside. His name was Skippy. Sometimes he got in trouble for going into the garden, but I knew Grandma had a lot of affection for him and often snuck him scraps of food when she was cleaning up the table. I don't know what ever happened to that dog.

***

Dad had two brothers. The youngest, Kyle, lived upstairs in Grandma's house. Mom hated his wife. She wouldn't say her name, just called her 'the redhead' and nearly spit when she said it. But her name was Lana and she and my uncle divorced a long time ago when I was still quite young. We completely lost touch with each other for many years, but we have reconnected recently and we find lots of things to talk about, many involving my mother or father or both. One story she relayed to me happened on a summer day when she walked across the field into our back yard. Aunt Lana was in her early twenties at the time and she was going to return a map my father had loaned her. Mom happened to be in the garden picking vegetables and she stood up and snarled, "What do you want?" "Hello Shirley. I just want to return this map to Bill." "You stay away from us and leave him alone!" My mother picked up a handful of dirt and threw it at her.

Uncle Kyle and Aunt Lana would have three children. Kevin was first. He eventually came to own the old Model A and he did an amazing job of restoring it, right down to new upholstery and historically correct colors on the exterior. When the work was complete, he proudly drove it every year in the Memorial Day parade that wove around the village streets we knew so well. When his parents divorced, Kevin remained with his father and had a very hard childhood, sometimes describing himself as his father's 'slave.' He was never allowed to have friends over, leave the yard except for school or church, or have any leisure time. Instead, he was made to do chores around the house and work in the garden. If Uncle Kyle was not pleased with him, Kevin often got the back of his father's hand, leaving the imprint of his watch on Kevin's skin. When he graduated from high school and wanted to get his own place, Uncle Kyle thought he could prevent Kevin from leaving. But my father intervened, telling his brother that Kevin was grown now and had the right to his own life. I never knew any of that until recently and I'm so sorry that my cousin had to grow up that way. He's a very quiet, unassuming, gentle human being.

A daughter came next for them, then another boy, who had encephalitis as a baby and was severely disabled. As was often the case with the disabled in those days, he was not kept at home, but instead lived out his life in a state-run facility. It was all very mysterious to me then. I knew he existed; I had seen him once. I also knew he was gone. Where was he? What happened to him? I never heard it discussed.

Dad's older brother lived a little farther away, not really within walking distance, and Dad was forbidden by my mother to go there. He is named after my grandfather, but he answers to various nicknames. Dad called him McGee; we kids always called him Uncle Jim. His wife's name is Gina and Mom hated her too. If Dad had to run to the store, Mom would make him take one of us kids to make sure he didn't stop at his brother's. I never understood it; it was just the way it was. I do not remember ever being in my uncle's house until after my mother died, but he and my aunt are wonderful people and we now have a good relationship. They are 94- and 95- years old and I love talking with them.

They had four kids. The oldest boy committed suicide, sitting on their basement stairs, when he was an adult. Although he was no longer living with them, he still had his workshop there, and they found him when they came home one day. He was a wonderfully talented artist and created beautiful pictures by etching them into glass. Local businesses would have his work built into their establishments in the form of windows, mirrors and glass doors. He had bipolar disorder and was on medication, but when he felt good he would stop taking it. That turned out to be a fatal mistake. Since we didn't see much of each other as kids, my one memory of him was how deep and husky his voice was. It didn't seem to fit a young boy. He would turn over rocks, looking for salamanders. When he found one, he would yell in delight in that man-voice of his, "Look! Look! I found a salamander!"

There were also two girls and another boy. The oldest girl is four years younger than me but my mother had decided in her own head that there was some kind of competition between us. I was smart and a good student but it was important to Mom that I was the smartest and the best. I have no idea what my cousin's grades were – I didn't really care – but when my report card came, Mom would go right over to Grandma's to show it to her to prove that I was the smarter one. "I bet nobody else gets grades like this!" she would say to Grandma. If she would just stop the comparisons! It was embarrassing and it made me feel bad. I wanted to get good grades and I wanted Mom to be proud of me, but I hated her using me to one-up my father's niece. So, I decided to remedy the situation. I began to fail. On purpose.

I couldn't keep that up for long though because I really did like school. When I graduated from sixth grade, I got an award for scholastic achievement. It was based on a test we had taken before the end of the school year. After the test results came back, my teacher called my parents in to meet with me. I had correctly answered a math question on the test that no student in sixth grade was expected to get right because it was beyond anything we had been taught. Did he think I had cheated somehow, I wondered? My teacher explained to my parents what the question had been and then asked me how I figured it out. When I told him, he said, "…but we didn't cover that this year. How did you know what to do?" Shrugging my shoulders, my response was, "I don't know, it just made sense to me." That was the simple truth. I had a good relationship with our elementary school principal and he had started calling me 'Miss Information' earlier in the year. When he presented me with the award at our sixth-grade graduation ceremony, he relayed that story to the audience and finished by smiling at me and saying, "Of course, I never told her if my nickname for her was two words or one word." I feigned an exasperated look and everyone laughed.

***

I do remember a few times having a big meal at Grandma's house on Thanksgiving or Easter, with Mom and Dad and one or both of Dad's brothers and their families. I figured Mom must have thought it was ok to spend time with them if it was a special occasion. Grandma would use her good china and the table would be loaded with delicious things to eat. When we walked into the house, the wonderful aromas greeted us and we couldn't wait to sit down and dig in. Halfway through one of those family dinners, I recall being very sleepy. The bedroom where my grandparents slept was right off the dining room so Dad lifted me up to the big, high, comfy bed and tucked me in under the covers. I can still remember feeling warm and safe and contented lying there and listening to the animated voices of my family on the other side of the wall. Occasionally, even now, if I can't sleep I try to recreate that scene and that feeling in my mind. It relaxes me.

Because Mom had such an outlandish dislike for Dad's family, she sometimes came up with wacky, illogical ideas about things they were doing behind her back. When Patty and I were little, Grandma often made dresses for us and most of the time we were dressed in identical outfits. Mom suspected Grandma was scrimping on the material used for our dresses so she could use the extra to make something for our cousins. "Look!" she would say. "This skirt is supposed to be fuller," or "These sleeves are supposed to be longer. You watch, one of those girls is going to have a dress just like yours." That never turned out to be true. Another time she thought Grandma was letting herself into our house, for some entirely unknown reason, when we weren't home. She asked our local Chief of Police how she could prove it. He brought over some bright blue powder and sprinkled it over the spare key that was kept in a little dish on a high shelf on the back porch. The theory was, when Grandma reached up to get the key, she'd get the powder on her hands. It was supposed to stain her hands and everything she touched, thereby leaving a trail. "I'm going to catch your grandmother in the act!" She warned us not to reach up there and touch it. My little-girl self wanted to cry out, "Mom, stop. Please stop. Grandma's nice. She doesn't sneak into our house." Nothing ever came of the key with the blue dye. I don't know how long it remained there, but the trap was a bust.

CHAPTER THREE

Mom's family was different from Dad's but I liked them too, except for one of Mom's brothers. Gram was less of a homebody than Grandma, more adventurous, more outgoing, more social. She even took a trip to Hawaii once, just her and her sister Emily. That impressed me; I didn't know anyone who had ever been to Hawaii, unless they were in the military at the time. It was so far away! I guess if I'd been asked to describe Gram then I would have said she was 'modern,' but of course that would have been the opinion of a girl growing up in a very rural part of the country, many years ago. She and my grandfather didn't own a house; they rented an upstairs apartment with a great screened-in porch off the kitchen. Because it was upstairs, it had a nice view. The man who owned the house, and lived on the other side of it, had honey bees out back. From Gram's porch I could see beyond the trees that lined the driveway and into the field where the bees were buzzing around their hives. Gram always had fresh honeycomb. We would cut off a chunk, put it in our mouths, suck out all the honey and then chew the wax that was left, like gum. I loved to stay at Gram's overnight during the summer so I could sleep on the porch. If I was mad at my mother, I would sometimes ride my bike to Gram's. Once in the winter I walked there through the snow. I walked the entire way, through fields and over roads, backward. As ridiculous as it sounds now, I thought if my footprints were facing the wrong way my mother wouldn't know where I'd gone. Gram taught me how to play Canasta, and then she taught my sister Patty. I sometimes drove her crazy when we played because I felt compelled to arrange the cards on the table every time it was my turn. They had to be spaced evenly apart, in nice straight rows. "Carol!" she would say. "For heaven's sake, just play!"

My grandfather was movie-star handsome, with thick black wavy hair, but he didn't engage much in conversation. If someone asked him a question, the most they usually got in return was a grumble. I called him 'Grumpy,' a name that only I used. He was a drinker and often away on lengthy fishing trips, which was just fine with Gram because when he was home he was abusive. I never witnessed it, but I heard about it. He was nice to me though, even funny sometimes, and I liked him. He was color-blind, and although neither my mother nor my brother could see red and green properly, I was told Grumpy couldn't see any color at all – only black and white and shades of gray. I delighted in showing him different colored marbles in a big glass bowl that Gram kept on a sideboard in the dining room. One at a time I would pick them up and he would guess at the color. Of course, he was always wrong and I would laugh every time. I suspect he could see more color than he admitted, but I think he enjoyed amusing me that way. I could also get away with tickling his feet when he was in his big, red recliner watching TV, even though he hated it and it made him jump. But when one of my cousins tried to do it, he yelled at her and told her to stop. "Carol does it," she would protest. "Why don't you holler at her?!" "Because Carol's my favorite." That statement now gives me pause.

Once, when I had the mumps, he sent me a get-well card and wrote on it, "To Mumpy from Grumpy." I still have it. He died of a sudden heart attack when he was sixty years old and I was just two weeks away from giving birth to my first child. He had joked with me that he was not old enough to become a great-grandfather. He never did. One of my sisters, who was still living at home when he died, told me recently that when Mom got the news about his death she fell to her knees on the kitchen floor, completely hysterical and inconsolable. My mother was not an emotional person; I honestly cannot remember ever seeing her cry. If she did show any emotion it was usually anger, displeasure, or jealousy. She was not particularly close to her father. She never had any real conversations with or about him that I was witness to. Occasionally she might mention that he was away on another fishing trip or relay something she'd heard about an incident at 'Lock 7,' where he worked. The lock was one of many on the Erie Canal system, used to raise or lower vessels from one water level to another. At most, if we were at Gram's and he happened to be home, Mom would talk to him about the weather or tell him something one of us kids had done. Or she would sit in the kitchen with Gram while Grumpy watched TV in the living room or went downstairs to putter around in the garage that was on the ground floor, under their apartment. So why this uncharacteristic outburst, this completely over-the-top reaction to his death? I don't believe it was grief.

***

Mom had three brothers and a sister, not counting two who had died as infants. Her youngest brother is just two years older than me and we went to the same school. He was more like a brother to me than an uncle, but I called him 'Uncle Reggie' when I saw him in the hallways, just to piss him off and embarrass him as he walked to class with his friends. I followed him around on his paper route and he didn't seem to mind, but he'd often buy himself an ice cream cone when he got paid, and when I told Gram, she said he had to buy me one too. I don't think that made him particularly happy. Reggie and Patty and I spent a lot of time together. In the winter we would go sledding or ice skating. In the summer we'd all walk down to the dam to go swimming. There was a long rope there that we could hold on to and swing out over the water, dropping at just the right second. There was also a big pine tree that had been sawed off leaving a platform of sorts on the top. Someone had nailed boards up the side of the tree that we used as a ladder. We'd stand on the platform and jump into the water. Some brave (or crazy) kids would stand on the top of the dam itself, but I never did that. I was afraid of falling off the wrong side. On Halloween, the three of us would take pillow cases and spend hours roaming the entire village. The pillow cases were Reggie's idea; they could hold a lot of loot, and they got so heavy we could barely carry them. Reggie also took me to my first scary movie. It was called "The Fly," and Vincent Price starred in it. After the show I was going to stay overnight at Gram's and sleep on that wonderful porch, but I was so terrified by the movie that I could not stay out there by myself after dark. I still don't like scary movies. When Reggie wasn't with his own friends, he was often challenging me to do things I might not have otherwise done. He was a bit of a dare-devil and I would push myself beyond the limits of common sense by copying him, even though he was older. I developed a derring-do attitude that has followed me all of my life and is probably why I broke a vertebra at the top of Killington trying to ski down a trail I had no business being on, and why, at the age of sixty-two, I celebrated my oldest son's fortieth birthday by jumping out of a plane with him. I have a picture of Reggie and me, taken just a few years ago on a very large roller coaster. In the photo, I am white-knuckling the grab bars, my eyes squeezed shut, my mouth wide open, screaming with delight. Reggie is sitting next to me, his hands in his lap, eyes looking straight ahead, perfectly calm. He looks like he's sitting at the dinner table, waiting to be served. It's a very funny picture, and remarkably reminiscent of the way we were as kids.

Mom's oldest brother shared Grumpy's love of booze and the two of them would spend long hours together in a bar on Main Street. His oldest daughter often had to walk to the bar to tell her father to come home. That uncle eventually caught his arm in a paper press at the paper mill where he worked. His arm was crushed and useless after that. He wouldn't let the doctors amputate it, so it atrophied and became a thin, lifeless thing that he carried around in a sling. I didn't like him much. He was gruff, intimidating, and sarcastic to me. He and his wife would come over often and play cards with Mom and Dad, but the only reason those visits were fun for me was that their three kids came too. The two oldest were girls with very long, straight blonde hair. I would brush their hair for a long time and sometimes style it into braids or ponytails. I loved that, and so did they. Eventually, my uncle and aunt both committed suicide. She was first and then, after being accused by police of causing her death, he shot himself with his hunting rifle. I'm sure somebody knows how and why all that happened, but I never did. I was grown then and my parents were away at camp. There were no cellphones; there was no such thing as email. I had to call the man who owned the campground and ask him to have my father call me back so I could tell him he needed to bring Mom home. I left it to Dad to tell Mom that her brother and his wife were both dead.

Rounding out my mother's family were her middle brother and her only sister. The brother and his wife had two boys. A third boy died as an infant, found dead in his crib of Sudden Infant Death Syndrome (SIDS). I was a couple of years older than the boys, and for a short time I was told to go over each day after school to fix them something to eat and 'watch' them until their mother got home from her job as a waitress. It made me mad because I had better things to do than babysit my cousins. By then, they certainly weren't babies, but it felt the same to me.

Mom's sister had eleven kids. Two girls and nine boys. That house was crazy! I loved going there. The oldest boy was one year older than me and the second one was one year younger than me. Those two were not her biological children. Their own mother had committed suicide when they were very young and my aunt became their mother when she married their father. Her last child was born two days before I gave birth to my second baby, in the same hospital. My family was a little wacky that way. And to make the situation even wackier, without knowing it, we gave our babies the same first and middle names, only in reverse order.

CHAPTER FOUR

We lived in a small, old, two-story house with three bedrooms that were upstairs and one bathroom that was downstairs. The kitchen was tiny. The bathroom was tiny. Actually, all the rooms were tiny. The gray linoleum on the dining room floor was worn so badly in places that the pattern was gone. The rug in the living room was threadbare and the old furniture was draped with fabric that had been sewn into some sort of 'fitted' cover. Curtains got swapped out twice a year. When the sheer summer curtains came out of storage, Mom would wash them and 'stretch' them on a big, adjustable wooden frame she had set up in the living room. It had tiny nails sticking out of it all the way around to hook the curtains on. As soon as they were dry, they were hung on the windows and the wooden frame went back into the cellar until next year. There were old radiators in most of the rooms, including the living room. Because we often wrestled and tumbled in that room, more than one of my siblings split their heads open on that radiator at one time or another.

There was one phone in our house, attached to the wall, and it rested on a little corner shelf Dad had built at the bottom of the stairway. Anyone who talked on the phone for longer than a minute or so usually just sat on the stairs. Any phone conversations were within hearing distance of everyone sitting in the living room. As a matter of fact, for a while we still had a 'party line' and had to listen for a second before dialing to make sure our neighbors weren't on the phone. If they were, we had to hang up and wait our turn, and they had to do the same for us. When I became a teenager, there was no more party line, but the phone remained in the same place and I found it annoying that I could not have a private conversation with a friend unless I left the house to see that friend in person.

Upstairs, Patty and I shared a bedroom on the left side of the house. The second bedroom was Mom and Dad's. It was on the right side of the house. Neither of these rooms had a closet. Mom and Dad had a chifforobe in their room for hanging garments, and when we were teenagers, Dad built a small closet in one corner of our bedroom so Patty and I had a place to hang our school clothes. I don't remember what the third bedroom was used for originally, but it was quite small and right in the front of the house, looking out over the front porch and onto the front yard. Eventually, it would be occupied by our only brother. In the back of the house was a small space that seemed fairly useless because you could only get to it by going through Mom and Dad's bedroom, or mine and

Patty's. On one side it had a slanting wall that followed the line of the roof. There was a window in the back, and if you were to climb out the window, you would be on a small, gently sloping roof that covered the back porch. Close to the porch roof was a tree with large, easy-to-climb branches. This was our fire escape plan. Dad made us recite it often: If we were on the second floor and the house was on fire and we could not go down the stairs, we were to go out that window, onto the roof, down the tree, and into the back yard. This little room was used for storage, but would eventually become a cramped, unlikely bedroom for the three youngest girls. The oldest of those three was ten years old when I decided to get married. As soon as she realized that I would be moving out, she could not wait to leave that cramped little room and her two baby sisters behind to take up my space in the bedroom with Patty.

Halfway down the cellar stairs there was a landing and a door that went outside. Our neighbor's driveway ran right along that side (the left side) of our house, and that's where the Freihofer's bakery truck would come one day each week to sell us coffee cakes, doughnuts, and other delicious treats. We'd run out the cellar door to greet him and Mom would usually let us choose what we wanted for the week. But only one thing, so we had to agree. The truck driver let us step right into the truck so we could examine all the possibilities before we made our decision. Our milk was also delivered directly to our house. The milkman would drive up our driveway, on the right side of the house, to access our back porch. Early in the morning, he would leave the bottles with the little cardboard caps inside the porch door so the milk wouldn't freeze in the winter. Patty and I always tried to get to the bottles first, sometimes even before Mom and Dad got up, so we could remove the caps and use a butter knife to retrieve the cream from the top. It was rich and delicious and silky smooth on our tongues.

We had a 'cold cellar' in the basement, a cool dark room where root vegetables were stored for the winter. Carrots, potatoes, and onions out of Dad's garden would last until next growing season. I liked going down into the cold cellar to dig around in a bushel basket full of dirt to pull out a few potatoes for dinner. They had to be kept cold and out of the light so they wouldn't grow 'eyes' and try to root in the dirt. If that happened, they would get soft and wrinkly and not be very good to eat. Another small room in the cellar contained wall-to-wall, floor-to-ceiling shelves where jars of canned vegetables and fruits were stored. Mom's wringer washer was down there too, as well as a big utility sink and an old washboard for stubborn stains or extra dirty clothes. Mom once caught her thumb in the washer's wringer and after that her thumbnail always looked like a tiny little washboard.

In the early years, our house was heated with coal. The delivery truck would come and the driver would open the designated basement window, extend the chute that came out of the truck, and proceed to dump a huge pile of shiny black nuggets into a small room in our cellar. The pile went almost up to the ceiling. When the furnace needed coal, Dad would go downstairs and shovel some in. My sister and I would sometimes take a few pieces of coal outside. It was great for writing on sidewalks and the foundations of houses, so we used it to play a game we called 'arrows.' One person would run around our house and several neighboring houses, drawing arrows to indicate which way she was going. The other person had to find her. The neighbors never seemed to mind and eventually the rain would wash away our arrows.

Across the road from our house was a piece of land that was jointly owned by our parents and two of our neighbors. Enough of it was cleared for us to use as a small softball field. We could pitch and hit and catch, but our bases were certainly closer together than those on a regulation field. Patty always pitched right-handed and batted left-handed. I could never figure out how she did that. There was wild asparagus that grew on the field and no matter how often Dad or one of the neighbors went over there to mow, the darn stuff wouldn't die. Eventually they gave up trying to get rid of it and we just ate it instead. Beyond the cleared field was a hill covered with thick woods. A well-worn path curved its way down to the bottom of the hill where there was a pretty stream. We often went down there and either waded in the water or challenged each other to make it across to the other side by walking on top of the slippery moss-covered rocks. Nobody ever succeeded, and more than once we went home wet, with our knees skinned and bruised. Sometimes I would pack myself a sandwich and go down there alone to just sit and think. The sound of the water rushing over the rocks was peaceful and relaxing. It was one of my favorite places to be.

Our back yard was narrow but very long, and adjoined the back yards of the people who lived on the next street over, including Grandma. It had a big old weeping willow tree that Dad often trimmed so the branches didn't drag on the ground and get wound up in the blades of his lawnmower. It was so pretty. Sometimes in the summer I would put a chair next to its trunk and sit there reading a book. There was also a grape arbor on which Dad grew purple grapes. They had seeds, but we didn't mind. We would hold a grape to our lips and squeeze. The grapes would pop out of their skins and right into our mouths. We discarded the skins and swallowed the rest whole, seeds and all. I can't imagine how many grape seeds we must have consumed in a summer. A cousin once told me with great authority that those seeds were all going into my appendix and someday it would explode. But, I reasoned, she was just a kid. What did she know?! Our neighbor had an apple tree in his back yard and my sister and I could pass what seemed like a whole afternoon in that tree, sitting as high up as we could go, eating apples, talking and playing silly games. We also played badminton and croquet. And way in the back part of our yard was Dad's garden. I wish I knew how many hours of his life were spent growing food for his family. Not only did he till it by hand every year, and plant the seeds and hoe the rows to keep the weeds down, but he schlepped water in buckets from the house back to the garden if we didn't get enough rain.

Our well was in the back yard too, close to the house. It was shallow and didn't hold much water, just like everyone else's. Our parents were always afraid of running out of water because that meant the fire department had to come with their big truck and fill up the well, and that cost money. So, we only bathed on Saturdays, in just a few inches of water. I remember sometimes needing to use the bathroom in the morning during the week but having to wait until Dad was finished getting ready for work by washing up in the sink. Sometimes, Patty and I would push aside the cinder block that covered the opening to the well, lie on our stomachs and peer inside. I don't know what we expected to see, but if one of us dropped a pebble, the ripples would tell us how far down the water was.

We had a nice old front porch that I loved on summer evenings when I needed some quiet time, and a small but pretty front yard. To one side was our long, narrow dirt driveway and just beyond it, bordering our neighbors' yard, was a strip of garden where Dad planted flowers. They were carefully planned so some would bloom in the spring, some in the summer and some in the fall. The early daffodils and tulips were colorful but my favorites were the poppies that always looked perfect just in time for Memorial Day. They weren't exactly orange and they weren't exactly red. They were big, bright, fragile-looking posies that swayed in the breeze and made me happy when I looked at them.

I always looked forward to Memorial Day. It was a day when our whole village came out to see the parade. Each church, community organization, and club spent months in preparation. People walked to their favorite spot along the parade route with their chairs or blankets and took up residence. Those who were lucky enough to live along the route sat on their front porches and invited others to join them. There were wonderful floats, school bands, horses, firetrucks, and police cars. Scouts and youth groups marched and threw candy to the cheering, flag-waving spectators. And of course, there were the veterans – proud, heads held high, marching in step in the regalia of their various branches of the armed forces. Dad and his brother were always among them, handsome in their uniforms. Mom, who was a member of the VFW Auxiliary, marched too. Patty and I would decorate our bicycles, weaving red, white and blue crepe paper through the spokes and attaching playing cards to the forks of the bikes with clothespins so they would make a clicking sound against the spokes as we rode alongside the parade. One year as Mom marched with the other ladies in their Auxiliary uniforms, she stumbled and fell. I didn't see it happen, but a lot of other people did, and I overheard her talking to Dad later that day. She was very upset because, she said, some people thought she'd been drinking. In fact, she told him, her legs had just suddenly and inexplicably 'turned to rubber' and collapsed underneath her.

CHAPTER FIVE

My sister and I found many ways to entertain ourselves, but sometimes the things we came up with got us into trouble, like the time I gave her a haircut. It was my idea, but she went along. To be fair, she was younger and inclined to do just about anything I suggested. I cut off her beautiful blonde curls – every one of them – and left her with very short, hacked-off hair. Then I hid under the dining room table where I thought my mother wouldn't find me. She did, and she was not happy! Another day, when she was mad at me for something, Patty scratched my name into an end table in the living room, hoping I would get yelled at. It worked temporarily and I got sent to my room with the usual, "You just wait until your father gets home!" but somehow Mom figured it out and I was exonerated. I really don't know how Patty had managed to do it in the first place without somebody catching her in the act, because it must have taken her a while. Mom covered the graffiti with a strategically placed doily, probably one my grandmother had crocheted, and set some kind of little knick-knack on top of it.

Patty was a funny, clumsy little kid. She was always making me laugh by running into things or falling down. Some nights she would fall out of bed and hit the floor with a thud. Then she would just get up and climb back into bed. One night at the dinner table, Dad was asking us about our day. All of a sudden, Patty was on the floor. No reason. She simply fell off her chair. I was laughing so hard I had tears in my eyes, but when she popped up and declared, "How 'boot dat?!" I think I wet my pants.

The two of us thought we were pretty clever, especially when we were in cahoots. One Christmas we woke up very early and could not go back to sleep. We weren't supposed to open presents until Mom and Dad were up, but certainly a little peek wouldn't hurt. We snuck down the stairs, our eyes wide and our hands over our mouths to remind ourselves not to talk. When a little peek led to uncontrollable curiosity, we came up with a plan. We would unwrap each package, take a look, then wrap it back up. Simple. I located the scotch tape in the kitchen drawer, just in case we needed it. We were careful to be very, very quiet. When we were done, we crept back upstairs and went to sleep. Mom and Dad were already in the kitchen fixing breakfast when we finally emerged. I can't imagine what they must have thought when they saw all the gifts under the tree in torn, crumpled paper and crooked ribbons, all held together with way too much tape, but they never said a word.

When I had just turned six and Patty was almost five, we decided it would be a good idea to cut the grass. We got our wagon and a small pair of pointy scissors that Mom kept in her sewing basket. I lay across the wagon in front of the house, feet sticking out one side and upper body sticking out the other side. I readied the scissors and Patty started to pull. We didn't get very far. After only a few snips, the wagon tipped over and I landed with the scissors sticking into the center of my chest. I jumped up from the ground and ran into the house bleeding, scissors in my hand. Mom took one look and frantically drove me to the bottom of our road where one of our two local doctors lived and worked on Main Street. The doctor told my mother I was very lucky; it could have been much worse. He pulled the wound together with a metal clamp and covered it with a thick bandage. The clamp had teeth and it hurt! I still have that scar. That same summer, Patty was riding her tricycle and we decided to take it for a spin up the road. She was peddling and I was standing on the back. Sometimes I had to help her out by putting one foot down on the road behind me and giving us a push. We passed a couple of houses and got to a place where the shoulder of the road dropped off into what used to be a farmer's field. A couple of feet down were the remnants of an old rusty barbed-wire fence that had once surrounded the field. Patty maneuvered too close to the edge and we toppled over, rolling down into the barbed wire. We walked the tricycle home, crying, with little bloody holes in our arms, backs and shoulders. They stung, like we'd been bitten by a bunch of angry bees. That little adventure cost our parents another doctor bill and cost us a couple of tetanus shots and a great deal of pain.

For every time Mom had an expected response to our antics, there would be another time when her reaction was completely over-the-top. Once, although I don't remember why, she shoved me onto my bed and started screaming, "You'd better be nice to me because someday you'll be crying 'Mommy, Mommy, Mommy' and I won't hear you because I'll be dead!" By the time she was done I was hysterical. That satisfied her and she walked out, leaving me there sobbing. She never did any of this stuff when Dad was around.

In retrospect, that incident may have been one of the reasons I began having nightmares, although I didn't connect the two and I never told anybody what Mom had said to me. I started waking up in the middle of the night, crying. Dad would come and sit on my bed. "What's wrong? Why are you crying?" "I had a dream that you and Mommy both died and I didn't know what to do." After about two weeks of that, Mom and Dad went together to talk to somebody at school and soon I had several sessions of 'counseling', once a week, during the school day. This was toward the end of my

Kindergarten year, so I was either five or just turned six. Eventually, the nightmares subsided. Surely, nobody, including my mother, ever thought she was the cause of my terror.

Except for some old fashioned over-the-knee spankings administered by our mother when we were little, we didn't often get hit. Mom tried to backhand Patty once in the kitchen for sassing her back, but Patty ducked and Mom slammed her knuckles into the door jamb. We both ran outside. And once I was standing on a dining room chair, facing a round mirror that hung on the wall. Dad was at the table doing some paper work. I was performing for myself in front of the mirror, but that wasn't unusual so Dad ignored me and went back to his papers. Soon I started singing and acting out a song I'd heard that day, doing my version of the hula: "In the middle of France, Where they don't wear any pants, But they do wear grass, To-oo cover up their..." WACK! Dad was out of his chair and smacked me squarely on my backside. "Where did you hear that?!" "Some kids were singing it at school today," I said, tears welling up in my eyes. I was trying hard not to cry. "Well, don't ever let me hear you say that again!"

We weren't always getting into mischief. There were times when we were called upon to do some things that required us to walk around town soliciting money, and we took our responsibility very seriously. I can think of two examples. The first was our yearly Sunday School picnic. We would be given a list of names and addresses of people who were members of our church. Then we would set out together, stopping at those houses and say, "Hello, we're soliciting for the Sunday School picnic." We would hold out our envelope and people would donate whatever they could afford, sometimes taking money out to make change. The second was selling poppies for Memorial Day. Dad would bring home a little round canister from the VFW and give it to us. This time there was no list of addresses; we stopped at every house. Some people would take a poppy and slide their donation into the little slot at the top of the can, some people would not want a poppy, but give a donation anyway. These little jobs were fun for us, but they also served to teach us how to talk to people we didn't know well, be polite, and be trustworthy. We also liked to do nice things for people sometimes, just because it made us feel good. On May Day, we would pick wildflowers, put them in little paper baskets, and hang the baskets on the front doors of our neighbors' houses. Then we'd ring the doorbell and run away. There was an old woman a few doors down that we would go to visit just because we knew she was lonely. There was nothing for us to do with her but sit and talk, so we never stayed long, but it seemed to make her happy that we stopped by. For birthdays, Valentine's Day, and Christmas, we would make our own cards with construction paper, crayons, paper doilies, and glue. Sometimes we made little gifts to go with them, depending on what materials we had available to us. And then there was our favorite good deed: 'breakfast in bed.' I have no clue where the idea originated or when it was first carried out, but we found it a fun thing to do on a Saturday morning. Mom and Dad often stayed in bed a little later on the weekends, so we were up before they were. We were still pretty young, but were learning to cook simple things. We'd get out eggs, bread, butter and jam. One of us would cook the eggs, the other would take care of the toast. We couldn't make coffee, but we knew how to fix tea, with sugar and a little milk. We didn't fill the cups too much, because we didn't want to spill anything. Then we would put it all on trays with napkins and forks, arranged just so, and carefully climb the stairs. We would present each of them with a tray, then exit their bedroom and close the door. We were so pleased with ourselves! The egg whites were probably runny, the yolks broken, and the toast sometimes a little burnt. But there was butter and jam, so how bad could it be? It makes me laugh now, because I'm sure, every time they heard us downstairs banging pans around in the morning, our parents said to each other, "Oh no, not again." But they always seemed appreciative. What's even funnier is that we were apparently unaware that Dad hated eggs.

Mom didn't exactly neglect her kids, but she did the bare minimum. And she was certainly not above getting us to do anything and everything she thought we could handle, especially if it was something she didn't want to do. During the summer after my Kindergarten year, my parents' only son was born. I was six and I had never seen a penis before, but Mom showed me how to care for the circumcision, removing the wet or soiled diaper, cleaning him, putting Vaseline on a gauze pad and wrapping it gently around the wound before putting on a clean diaper. That's when I learned how awful a tiny baby's dirty diaper can smell! Ugh! Belly bands were common then, narrow strips of cotton that would wrap around an infant's tummy and be secured by tying the attached strings. Their purpose was to protect the thick stump of the umbilical cord until it dried up and fell off. Every time a diaper was changed, the belly band was also wet and needed to be changed. Then the used diaper had to be rinsed out and put into the diaper pail to soak. After I performed the task a few times under Mom's supervision, if she was busy doing something else, she let me take care of him. In those days there were only cloth diapers and diaper pins, and I didn't dare stick him! I learned to put my hand between his skin and the diaper as I carefully pushed the pin through the cotton.

Somehow, Mom had acquired a pretty blue parakeet named Davey. Davey was a girl, but that wasn't known until after she was named, so the name stuck. Mom let Davey out of her cage one day and the bird flew into my brother's bassinet, landing on his blanket. His little hand reflexively clamped onto the bird's tail and the bird quickly flew away, leaving several of her tail feather still in the baby's tight grasp. The bird had trouble balancing on her perch after that, and often stood on the floor of her cage until she was able to grow some new feathers. Patty and I laughed at the way she teetered around. But most of the time we weren't very interested in the bird, so I don't remember anything else about Davey; I think she must have been given away.

Nineteen months after Brandon was born, my parents' third daughter came along and I became her little mother. I was eight. She came to me when she was hurt or sad. I read to her, combed her hair, helped her pick out her clothes, and kissed her boo-boos. There was a silly little story called "The Teeny Tiny Woman" that she loved, and I read it to her over and over again. She snuck into my bed at night, coming through the door that connected my bedroom with the little room in the back of the house, and curled up next to me. When she was older and going to a school dance, I did her hair for her, tucking pink ribbons into her blonde curls. She was always a sweet kid and she looked so pretty.

She was excited about having a date, a boy in her class who was coming with his father to pick her up. After she put on her dress, Mom came into the room and looked her up and down. She said, "I guess he couldn't find anyone else to go with him," and walked back out. Dana has blocked nearly all memories of our mother out of her consciousness. She told me long after she was out on her own, "I haven't felt taken care of since you got married and moved out of Dad's house."

Brandon was a rambunctious little boy, always running around and seldom pausing for more than a minute or two. One day, something happened that made us all very sad. We always had cats when we were growing up. They started out as strays but, after some begging, we were occasionally allowed to keep one. They were always free to roam outside and they never went to the vet to be 'fixed', so there would often be kittens. Patty and I loved the furry, playful little babies but we knew we couldn't keep them. We were once sitting on the living room floor with a new litter in a shallow cardboard box lined with an old baby blanket. We would have to give them away soon, but for now they were ours! Our little brother came running through the room. He didn't see the kittens and he stepped squarely on one of them. Dad heard us scream and he appeared immediately, instantly assessing the situation and quickly removing the lifeless little creature. When he returned, he simply said there was to be no mention of it to Brandon. Poor kid already felt bad and it was, after all, not his fault.

Around this same time, one day when Mom was upstairs cleaning, my brother had a little accident that could have ended very badly. Mom had a bedroom window open and she kept going back to it to shake out her dust mop. Brandon was wandering around, looking for something to get into and he climbed on top of the radiator that was in front of that window. Quicker than a flash, out he went. There was a concrete sidewalk down there, covered by about two inches of snow – certainly not enough to afford any cushioning. Mom stood in the middle of the room, frozen. She couldn't even bring herself to go to the window. There was no crying coming from outside. I flew down the stairs and threw the front door wide open, about to run to my brother. But there he stood on the porch, unshaken, unperturbed. Mom was still upstairs, completely silent, as Brandon asked me if I would make him a peanut butter and jelly sandwich.

In the winter Patty and I sometimes skated on a little pond several houses down, way back in a field. Dad always insisted at the beginning of the season that we go over, knock on the owners' door and ask permission to skate there. They were two elderly sisters. They knew us, of course, and they always said yes. We would put some object –

usually a hat or somebody's scarf – on the ice and practice jumping over it while singing "Winter Wonderland" or "Let It Snow." We could spend hours outside in the cold. Our feet would be frozen, our fingers would be numb, and our teeth would chatter, but we never wanted to go in if we were having fun. Patty and I wondered why anyone would have a pond way back there in the middle of a field that they never seemed to use for anything. We had fun on it in the winter, but as far as we knew, nobody swam in it in the summertime. Maybe it wasn't deep enough. In a conversation with Dad long after I was grown, he told me that if we'd ever gone back there when the weather was warmer (we were never allowed to do that), the unfrozen water itself would have answered my question. It was sewer water.

Although she was younger, Patty was always the brave one. I had an unreasonable fear of the dark, clowns, and Santa Claus, and I would hold her hand to give myself courage. Certainly, I wasn't afraid of the idea of Santa, but no way did I want to go to a department store and sit on his lap. "Come on, Carol," she would say, pulling me along, "it's just Santy Claus. Don't you wanna tell him what you want?" Together we played tag and hide-and-seek. We challenged each other to coloring contests to see who could make the best outlines and shadows using only crayons. We walked or rode our bikes to the school playground where we would stand upright on top of the 'monkey bars' and walk across them, rung by rung, with nothing but our balance and our determination to keep us from crashing to the ground. Nearly everyone knew who our parents were and where we lived, so we were usually free to roam and explore as long as we were home when the five o'clock whistle blew.

One warm summer Sunday, dressed early for Sunday School, Patty and I took off for a walk. We wandered down to the dam and I decided to take a quick swing on the rope before heading back home. I'd done it a hundred times. I just wouldn't let go over the water. I'd swing out and back and put my feet on the ground. Not this time! I fell in and had to walk back home with my Sunday best, including my patent leather shoes, soaking wet. I don't remember if I got in trouble over that, but I'm pretty sure I didn't make it to Sunday School that day. Later that summer Dad built us a playhouse, complete with a real little latching door, shutters on the windows, a front porch and shingles on the roof, but I think he enjoyed building it more than we enjoyed playing in it. He teased me, saying next time I got dressed early on a Sunday morning, instead of walking to the dam, maybe I should walk out to the playhouse and read a book. Patty and I played in it occasionally, but we much preferred being out in the open, running and climbing and wearing ourselves out.

Mom once allowed me to take in a cat that I was particularly attached to. I had been sneaking food to her for quite a while so my parents relented and allowed me to bring her inside. I named her Queenie. I spent a lot of time with her sitting on my lap while I read or did schoolwork. At night, she slept next to me or at the foot of my bed. She was an affectionate cat and she always came to me when I called her. She was warm and her fur was soft, and she always purred when I petted her. It was calming and comforting to me. One night she was left outside and got into a fight with another cat. It wasn't unusual; we had heard the terrible sounds of cats fighting many times. But this time she came home missing an eye. I was beside myself, and Dad felt sorry for her and was worried the wound would get infected, so he took her to the local vet. When she came home, the place where her eye had been was sewn permanently closed. I loved Queenie, and after that, I was even more attentive and diligent about taking care of her. Then one day, my mother told Dad she wanted to "get rid of that cat." There was no reason given, but she had made up her mind. They would put her in the car and take her to the shelter. Someone would give her a nice home. "No, they won't," I shouted. "She's old. She's only got one eye. They'll kill her." I was sobbing now, hysterical, but Mom always got her way. She did not try to console me and Dad did what he always did – he quietly complied with her wishes. He scooped up the cat and instructed me to stay home until they got back. "No! I'm going with you!" I held Queenie in the back seat and cried all the way to the shelter, my head bent over her, my tears wetting her fur. I thought they would change their minds and turn around. But Queenie was left at the shelter and we went home. I was never given an explanation. I tried to figure out a way to get to the shelter and bring her back. I would hide her in my room and they wouldn't know. But there was clearly no path to success, so I gave up the idea. I was miserable for days but my grief went unnoticed – or at least, unacknowledged. I don't know how many times in the next few weeks I told my mother, silently, that I hated her.

The farmer's field down the road where Patty and I had tangled with the old barbed wire fence had a long, steep hill and Dad took us there one day to go sledding. The snow was several days old and weather conditions had been just right to create a hard, icy surface on top. Patty flew down the hill first. It was fast! Then it was my turn. Dad would come down last. There were no plastic sleds back then. We had a toboggan, but this day we were using sleds with metal runners on the bottom. I jumped onto my sled, landing on my stomach, and almost immediately the runners broke through the hard surface and stuck into the soft snow below, stopping it short. But my body kept going. My face scraped across the crusty snow and when I finally came to a stop and got up, I realized it felt strangely numb. I thought it was just from the cold. I reached up and touched my cheek. My mitten was full of blood. Dad was right behind me and I looked at him, panicked. I said, "What's bleeding?!" His simple, calm response was, "You took all the skin off your face." We waited for Patty to finish trekking back up the hill with her sled, then we all walked home. Another trip to the doctor. The next day I had school, and my face was so red and oozy and swollen that I didn't even look like me. Eventually a thick scab formed and the doctor slowly, methodically peeled it off. He said if he didn't remove the scab, my face would be scarred. But oh, how it hurt! It was hard to sit still and allow him to finish. Over the years, with six kids in the family, there were many accidents and injuries. We were kids just being kids.

My brother also had a sledding incident, but on a different hill. It was a fairly gentle slope but very wide. Lots of kids were there on a snowy day. At the bottom, right in the middle, was a telephone pole, but with all that space it was easy to avoid. Or so you would think. Brandon had built a jump out of snow and had taken several runs over it. The more it packed down, the faster it got. Dad loved snow. He loved helping us build giant snowmen and he loved to go sledding and tobogganing with us, but on this particular day he must have been working because only Patty and I were there with Brandon. He went to the very top of the hill, got a running start, threw himself onto his sled and whizzed down to the jump. He hit it perfectly and launched into the air with a big smile on his face. Then something went wrong. He twisted in the air and came down crooked. He didn't tip over but he flew off course, heading directly for the telephone pole. There wasn't enough time for him to think about rolling off the sled; he hit the pole head-on. Patty and I ran to him but we were horrified when he turned around and looked at us. His mouth was bloody and he was missing a front tooth. Once again, we walked home with a battle-scarred warrior.

I watched Patty do a face plant too, but it was not in the winter. The two of us were riding our bikes. We'd gotten pretty good at riding all around town without holding on to the handlebars, even around corners. But that day Patty lost control. We'd been going pretty fast and when she fell, she got all scraped up, mostly her face. Her lip was puffed up and bleeding and her forehead and one cheek were full of cuts and scrapes and little bits of embedded gravel. One shoulder hurt and she was shaking and crying. She looked awful! As she sat on the side of the road holding her shoulder, I encouraged her to get back on her bike, and ever-so-slowly we rode home together. At least she still had all her teeth.

I was always the one in the family who didn't need much sleep. Even as a kid I could stay up late and get up early without much trouble. Once in a while in the summer we would all pile into the car and go to a drive-in movie. It was one of the few things my parents could afford to do with all of us together. Once inside the fence, there was a playground to keep us occupied until it got dark enough for the movie to start. Sometimes we were allowed to go to the concession stand and get popcorn. Mmmm. You could smell it popping before you even got to the building. Once back in the car, we'd all maneuver until everyone could see the screen. Usually it meant not being in a very comfortable position, but we didn't mind. There were blankets and pillows in case anyone got cold or tired, and soon the younger kids would be asleep. Then Patty. Then Mom. Eventually, even Dad succumbed and I would be the only one still awake. I couldn't understand how they could fall asleep without knowing how the story ended. As people started their cars and turned on their headlights, I would shake Dad's shoulder and say, "The movie's over. Time to go home."

One day Dad surprised us all with something way better than a drive-in movie – our first television! The only other people I knew who had one were my aunt and uncle, and I guess Dad didn't want to be outdone. The picture was black and white and very small, but we were thrilled! There were three stations. If you stayed up late enough, you could see the station you were watching sign off, because there was no TV broadcasting at night. The TV relied on cathode ray tubes and they sometimes burned out. When that happened, there would be no TV until Dad could get a new tube to replace the bad one. Another annoyance was that the picture had to be constantly adjusted. Sometimes it would turn to all static, or other times to rolling horizontal lines. Next to the volume knob there was one you could turn to get the picture back into focus, but sometimes it seemed as though it had to be done every few minutes. Dad was so proud of that TV! We kids loved it, but Mom was afraid to touch it. There was nothing complicated about operating it, but she would always ask one of us to do it for her. There were so many good, fun, family shows on TV back then, and with only one TV in the house, everyone watched together.

Patty and I were assigned the chore of clearing the dinner table and washing and drying the dishes every night. We had that job for years and we actually enjoyed doing it. Each night we'd first argue over who would wash and who would dry, but once that was settled, we spent the rest of the time laughing and telling each other funny stories and jokes. Patty was the queen of puns and she'd say the funniest things! We'd have contests to see who could hold her breath the longest, using the kitchen clock to time ourselves. Before we even knew it, the dishes were done and put away.

Another chore that I enjoyed and often volunteered to do was hanging freshly washed clothes out to dry. We had no clothes dryer, so no matter the season, they had to be hung. The clothesline was long. It started from a window on the back porch and went out to a tree in the back yard. It was on pulleys so you could roll it out as you hung the clothes. Sheets and towels, kids' clothes, diapers, Dad's shirts, Mom's blouses – everything smelled so fresh when you brought it back in. In the winter each item would freeze and become stiff as a board, but once you removed the clothespins and brought it back inside, it thawed out very quickly so you could fold it and sort it into neat piles. I found it very satisfying.

We were poor, but so were most of the other families in our village, so we didn't feel as if we were missing out on anything. We rarely got new things and we always took care of what we had because if something got lost or broken, there would be no replacement. Most of my school clothes were bought second-hand from another girl in my class who was larger than me. When she outgrew them, I got them. When I outgrew them, my sister Patty got them. Ice cream was only for birthdays and eating out meant stopping for a fast-food burger once a year on our way to camp. My only bike was the one that had been my Mom's when she was a kid. Grumpy repainted it and wrote my name on the crossbar. I rode that bike a lot!

Once, I was flying down the road toward Main Street. The hill was steep, my feet were off the pedals and my hair was blowing in the wind. Just before I got to the bottom, I slammed on the brakes. As the wheels stopped turning, the bike fell apart underneath me. Someone who saw what had happened stopped his car, loaded up the pieces of what used to be my bike and drove me back up the hill to our house. Mom saw him drive in, and when he started pulling familiar bike parts out of his trunk, she thought I'd been hit by a car. She came running out of the house in a panic, but was relieved to see me getting out of the car, still in one piece.

When we'd outgrown our neighbors little 'skating pond' we were allowed to skate at the dam. We had come up with a contest of sorts, one that we particularly liked. One of us would start near the dam and skate as fast as we could, heading up the creek. When we reached a long vine hanging down out of the trees, we'd grab hold, swing way up into the air, twist ourselves around and come back down to be propelled by the momentum back in the direction from which we had come. Another of us would measure, to see who could go the farthest without picking either foot up off the ground after letting go of the vine. That vine had taken us on a lot of rides, but one day when I was about six feet off the ground, the vine broke. I landed on the ice on my elbow and cracked the bone in my forearm.

It hurt a lot and I didn't skate for a few weeks because I was afraid of falling on my arm again.

We also skated at the old brick yard. It was a little farther away and a bit of a walk, but it was a great place to skate! Men from the local Kiwanis Club would flood it every year and make sure it was always cleared of snow. It was big enough to allow a long line of skaters, holding hands, to whip the person on the end around in a circle. Sometimes we'd get going so fast we'd let go and fly off the end of the line. The Kiwanis would occasionally hold organized races, and there was always a big barrel with a roaring fire to stand by and warm our hands. I could skate pretty fast, but I never won a race. Still, it was a lot of fun. I learned to skate backwards and spin in a circle, and I was pretty good at hockey stops, but that was the entirety of my ice-skating repertoire. That brick yard was just one of the remnants of industry in our little town. There had once been a piano factory too, and the sky-high round chimney still stood straight up in the air, although the rest of the factory was long since gone.

CHAPTER SIX

When I was young, Mom was always in dresses and, often, high heels. And every day, without fail, she wore bright red lipstick. I guess she was pretty, but I never thought of her that way. As a teenager and young adult, I looked amazingly like she had at my age, but half a foot taller and minus the red lipstick. She always seemed unsatisfied with the life she had, as if she deserved something better. One day when she was in a foul mood, she yelled at no one in particular that she was leaving and never coming back. If I had to guess I'd say we were 10, 9, 4 and 2. She walked out through the back porch and slammed the door behind her. Of course, Dad wasn't home; she never would have let him see the stunts she pulled. The little kids were crying and I was in a panic, not knowing what to do. I ran to a window that looked out on the back stairs. From there I could see the garage and I wanted to know if the car was pulling out of the garage and onto the driveway. But Mom wasn't in the car; she was standing on the stairs, her ear against the door, smiling while she listened to the bedlam going on inside. Another time, when I walked to a friend's after school, she called the friend's house. I hadn't come home right away, and she was correct in assuming that's where I had gone. Mom knew my friend's mother worked and would not be at home. When a girl's voice answered the phone, my mother let her have it. She didn't like any of my friends. Truth be told, I don't think she wanted me to have any friends. She called the girl all kinds of names and told her, "I don't want my daughter hanging around with you. Tell her to come home right now." I didn't know about the phone call until I got to school the next day because apparently when Mom was reading the number in the phone book, her eyes had skipped down a line and she had called another girl, an older girl a grade above me, by mistake. I was thankful that the recipient of my mother's phone call was discreet when she told me about it. Of course, I couldn't wait to tell my mother what she had done. She was clearly taken aback and I was satisfied to see a hint of confusion, then embarrassment on her face. She knew who the other girl was. But she wouldn't acknowledge what I was saying, or offer any kind of an apology. She just went on about her business, as if I wasn't even talking to her.

Dad didn't escape Mom's ire either. When he was at one of his Air Force Reserve meetings, she sat with us at the dinner table and told us he was not really at a meeting, he was out with his girlfriend. Who says that to their kids?! I guess she didn't realize that by then we knew she was full of shit. She was a lousy housekeeper and a terrible cook, although she did have a few recipes that I still like. There's an old saying, "sweep the dirt under the rug." She literally did that. She would pick up the edge of the rug in our living room and sweep dirt under it instead of getting the dust pan and picking it up. It was usually just as Dad was driving up the driveway and, no matter how many times I watched her do it, I still couldn't believe my eyes. She was jealous of the fact that Dad went to the office every day, because she knew there were women there. She would yell and make up stories and unkind names for all the people she imagined were doing her wrong. She was like a bully on a playground. Dad never yelled back and he never seemed to let Mom's accusations get to him. I don't think I ever heard him curse. He would say, "Your mother has green eyes," inferring that her jealousy and mistrust of him were not things over which she had any control.

I recall the afternoon that Mom decided to take up smoking. She had the ironing board set up where she always put it, in the dining room. There was enough room there for her to set the laundry basket on the floor next to her, she could stack folded items on the table as she finished ironing them, and there was an electrical outlet within easy reach. I was sitting at one end of the table doing schoolwork. She started to mumble about being mad at Dad for something. She clearly wanted an audience and, besides her, I was the only one in the room. As I looked up, she pulled a pack of cigarettes out of the pocket of her sweater, put one between her lips and lit it. I couldn't believe my eyes; neither of my parents smoked.

"What are you doing?!"

"Getting even with your father."

"For what?"

"None of your business."

"That doesn't make any sense. How can you get even with somebody by smoking cigarettes? And besides, you look ridiculous."

She tried to inhale and started to cough, which led to her choking violently and running to the bathroom. That was the last time I ever saw her pick up a cigarette.

Mom accused me of stealing; she accused me of lying. She accused me of all sorts of things. She rifled through my schoolbooks and notepads, looking for some terrible thing I or someone else may have scribbled. I had a few pen pals, mostly kids I had met at camp, and if I got a letter in the mail I could often tell it had been opened and resealed before Mom handed it to me. I sought the counsel of a friend's father. He was the director of our church's youth choir and a music teacher at a neighboring school. He was kind and patient, and when I told him how much my mother's accusations hurt and infuriated me, he said, "Don't let your mother push you over the edge. Don't become what she accuses you of being." It was excellent advice and I never forgot it.

Mom was not the kind of mother we could go to if we needed to talk about a problem or a boyfriend or a personal concern. We learned early on that confiding in her only led to being criticized, ridiculed, or berated in some way. She clearly enjoyed making people unhappy or hurting their feelings. It was like a sport for her; she seemed to find it satisfying. One summer morning she told us we were going to camp. Dad was at the office and we were to be ready when he got home. We were all excited and I began to do what had become my responsibility – packing for the younger kids. It was my job to know what they needed and it would be my fault if we got there and I had forgotten something. Clothes, bathing suits, jackets, pajamas, underwear and socks for each of them. And diapers and rubber pants for the youngest. For those of you who have no idea, rubber pants were put on over cloth diapers because cloth diapers got really wet, and so did everything they came in contact with. The others helped by packing up things that they wanted to take, like peanut butter and jelly sandwiches to eat on the way, favorite beach towels, toys and games. Those who were old enough also helped by carrying the things I was gathering out to the car and putting them in the trunk. We were ready! Then she pulled one of her classics. With a hint of a smile on her face she said, "I've changed my mind. We're not going." The younger ones cried out of disappointment. I quietly unpacked, unsurprised. She never had any intention of going anywhere.

There was a time that I was so angry with my mother that I jumped on my bike and tore across our front yard and onto our neighbors' dirt driveway, on my way out to the road and to some unknown destination. In shorts and a t-shirt, I was standing up on the pedals to facilitate speed. Just as I made a sharp left turn from the edge of our lawn onto their drive, my front tire skidded on the gravel and I went down, sliding along on my left hip and thigh. I could barely get up. Mom was on the front porch watching, but didn't say a word. The whole upper part of my left leg was devoid of skin and full of embedded pieces of dirt and gravel. I knew I had to clean it; I knew it was going to hurt like hell. I moved my bike to the lawn, limped past Mom into the house and into the bathroom, closing the door behind me. I was really hurting, but what hurt even more was that she had seen it happen. I knew she was smirking on the inside. It must have taken a half hour for me to gingerly pick all of the dirt out and clean the wound, wincing with pain the whole time. I wore loose cotton skirts for a while until a scab formed, but it hurt for a long while. I never mentioned it and neither did Mom. I wish I had learned how to react differently to her. I wonder what would have happened if I had tried to talk to her instead of flying off on my bike, retreating to the woods, or running off to Gram's or a friend's house. Would it have made a difference? Would she have taken a step back and talked about her reasons for being so volatile and hurtful? Would she have revealed anything that would shed some light on what went on inside her head?

She sometimes had 'visitors' at the house while Dad was at work and we were in school. Well, at least one. I suspect one other. We would get off the school bus and we knew the local yokel chief of police was there because the police car would be in the driveway. He was the one who put the blue powder on the key as a trap for my grandmother. If he wasn't there, she was talking to him on the phone. It was easy to tell because of the way she talked and the things she said. His daughter was in my class, so just to be a smart ass one day I walked by her and up the stairs, yelling over my shoulder, "Tell him to say hi to Charlene for me." She gasped. A few days later I told my dad what I suspected. Maybe he already knew. I asked him why he didn't leave her. I felt so bad for him and so resentful of her. I guess it didn't occur to me that if he left her, I'd lose him too. But as he always did, he quietly repeated one of his well-worn responses, "Let's not rock the boat." Another of his oft-used phrases was, "Let's not make your mother angry." It was infuriating.

My mom had only three friends that I remember. The first was her sister. When we were away at camp, they would keep in touch by writing letters to each other. Most of the time I didn't know what they wrote about, but sometimes there would be a new recipe in the envelope that Mom would try out on us. The second was her Aunt Corinne, who was her age and with whom she had always been best friends. Aunt Corinne stood up with Mom when she and Dad got married. Mom confided in her often and sometimes took us to Aunt Corinne's house where they would sit and talk over a cup of tea or a glass of lemonade while we kids played. Sometimes Mom would rub her left arm and complain to Aunt Corinne that it ached all the time and she couldn't find a way to make it stop. Once in a while she would do the same thing at the dinner table at home and tell Dad that the constant, nagging ache was driving her crazy. It didn't happen a lot, but I observed it often enough to wonder what was wrong with her arm. Her third friend was a woman in the neighborhood with whom she had endless gossipy phone conversations. The conversations were daily, long, easily overheard and about only one thing: tearing other people down. Family members, neighbors, people at church, people at school. Nobody was exempt. It became clear to me that Mom had very low self-esteem and it made her feel better about herself to pretend that other people were beneath her. This one wore ugly clothes. That one never combed her hair. Another one had stupid children or a lazy husband. And oh, doesn't whats-her-name have more than just that one old sweater? Or, did you taste those awful cookies so-and-so made for the church picnic? Aside from gossiping, I was only aware of two things that my mother liked to do. She liked to iron clothes and she liked to mow the lawn. Of course, back then we had a push mower. No gas motor, no electric motor, just good old-fashioned muscle power. I never could figure out why she thought either of those things was fun.

Mom's inexplicable displeasure never waned, and for a while she seemed to take delight in burning things. We recycled glass and cans and newspapers, and garbage was composted, but like all of our neighbors, we had a big metal burning barrel out back where papers and cardboard and such were disposed of once a week. Long before, each time he was away for one of his two-week active duty stints, Dad wrote letters to Mom every day he was gone and drew a cartoon on every envelope. Patty and I had loved seeing those envelopes come in the mail. Mom kept them in a bundle on a shelf in her bedroom. The cartoons were funny and they made us laugh. Later, in one of her snits over who-knows-what, she took them out back and unceremoniously burned them all. When he was in Okinawa, Dad had created two very large, incredible charcoal drawings. I remember he kept them rolled up in a big cardboard tube and locked in a footlocker. One was a very detailed picture of an army tank, the other of an Okinawan woman with the pained expression of someone who had seen horrible things. They also went up in flames. At her insistence, our piano got dragged out back and burned. Mom had played it when she was younger, but she said it was old and it didn't work anymore, so it had to go. I loved that piano. It was old, but there was nothing wrong with it. I played it nearly every day, working my way through the stacks of sheet music she had collected over the years. But that didn't matter to her; she wanted it gone. Dad complied. Then a few years later, when he no longer needed them, Dad came home one day to find she'd even burned his Air Force uniforms.

***

To be fair, time with our mother wasn't always unpleasant; sometimes she was nice, and she could even be funny. She often mixed up the first letters of words in a sentence and we would all burst out laughing, including her. She'd say things like, "He did a therrible ting." Or "Hand me that loaf of brye read." I don't know why it happened; sometimes her brain just scrambled the letters up.

She would play Scrabble with us even though she couldn't spell worth a darn and knew we would tease her unmercifully, and she liked Canasta. She was pretty good at that. We made fun of her color-blindness because sometimes it would cause her to do odd things. Dad was going to paint the back room where all of our toys were kept. Either it was tan and he had bought pale green paint, or just the opposite. Mom decided to surprise him and do it herself before he got home from work. When we walked in from school, she couldn't wait for us to see what she had done. We looked in the room and couldn't control ourselves. She had missed spots everywhere. She couldn't see the difference between the two colors. She laughed too, although her own eyes would offer her no proof that she'd done such a lousy job. The floor in the bedroom that Patty and I shared was covered with different colored linoleum tiles, patched together in a design in the center of the room. Red, green, black and yellow as I recall. Either Patty or I spilled a bottle of mercurochrome and, knowing how quickly it stained everything it touched, we yelled for Mom. She busied herself cleaning it up, but when she was done there was still quite a lot of splatter left. She could not see the red against some of the colors on the floor. Once again, we were happy to tell her what a terrible job she'd done. This time she threw up her hands in mock defeat, handed us some rags and a bucket of soapy water and told us to finish it ourselves.

She could also be forgiving if something happened that was obviously unintentional. Dad's birthday was coming up and a local grocery store had a giveaway for a birthday cake from their bakery. All you had to do was put your name in the box and hope you were picked. We'd never had a store-bought birthday cake. She was lucky that day; her name was drawn and she came home with a beautifully decorated cake that said, "Happy Birthday Dad." She sat it on the dining room table but I knew she wanted it to be a surprise. She was busy in the kitchen when I saw Dad turn into the driveway. I quickly grabbed the box containing the cake so I could hide it, but in my haste, I slipped and dropped it. The cake was smashed, still in its box. I was so upset! I ran up to my room, slammed the door, collapsed onto my bed, and pulled my pillow over my head. But Mom sent one of my sisters to tell me to come down for supper. When it was time for dessert, Mom explained to Dad what had happened, produced the cake, stuck a candle in it, and we ate it anyhow. After singing Happy Birthday, of course.

Dad gave me a glimpse of yet a different side of my mother after she died. During all his travels in the early part of his military career, he had bought her a jacket and had it sent to her. It was thigh-length, made of very light-weight cream-colored wool and on the back was an intricately embroidered Mexican scene. She had loved it and it still hung in their closet more than fifty years later. He showed me a picture he had taken of her many years before, in the back yard of the house where I grew up; I had seen the picture before. She was wearing the jacket, standing at an angle which allowed the embroidery on the back of the jacket to show, coyly looking over her shoulder at the camera. She was wearing her trademark high heels and her legs were bare up to the bottom of the jacket. Dad said to me, with a twinkle in his eye, "Do you know what your mother was wearing under that jacket? Nothing."

CHAPTER SEVEN

As far back as I can remember, Sundays were spent at church. Our mother didn't go very often, but our father was very involved, and from a young age we went to Sunday School every week. When we were old enough, we stayed after Sunday School and attended church service with Dad. I loved to sing and joined the junior choir. Then the adult choir. At one point, my Sundays looked something like this: Sunday School, church service, home for dinner, back to church in the evening for Catechism class followed by Youth Fellowship. Dad was always a member of the Church Consistory. A couple of times, when for some reason our Minister could not preach, my father got to write and preach the sermon. I was very impressed, watching him up there from my seat in the congregation. For many years he was also Treasurer. Patty and I often sat with him and other Consistory members after the service was over while they counted the offertory money and bundled it for deposit. Sometimes they let us help.

I met a lot of people through the church. For six years, Patty and I were gifted by a couple in our community with the money to attend Camp Fowler for a week each summer. It was a great place in the Adirondacks, for children whose families were connected with the Reformed Church in America. I looked forward to it every year and there was nothing about it that I didn't like. Even the rock-hard bunk beds and the ice-cold showers in our cabins didn't bother me because the rest of the experience was so wonderful. There were services in the beautiful chapel and prayers before meals, but much of the week was simply about kindness and fellowship and having fun with friends both old and new. The lake was spectacular, there were lots of fun activities, and everyone gathering together for a meal was an event in itself. There was kitchen staff, of course, but the campers all chipped in to set and clear tables together. There were skits and talent shows, and there was lots of music and singing. A week at Camp Fowler always left me feeling happy and inspired. Patty and I both made some good friends there with whom we would correspond throughout the year. I met my first serious boyfriend there, too. He eventually became a minister, as did a couple of other guys I dated.

At home, Sunday dinner was usually fried chicken and mashed potatoes, my favorite meal. I not only liked to eat it; I enjoyed cooking it. So, after church I often volunteered to bread and fry the chicken, peel and mash the potatoes. I would put some flour in a paper bag, add salt and pepper, and then shake each piece of chicken in the bag to coat it before putting it in the hot oil. When it was cooked just right, I'd place the hot, crispy, golden pieces on a paper towel and then onto a serving dish. The potatoes were mashed with butter and milk until they were free of lumps. After scooping them into a bowl, I'd sprinkle a little parsley on the top to make them look nice. Someone else would generally take care of the vegetables and setting the table. In the summer the vegetables were fresh from the garden, in the winter they came from our stash of home-canned goods in the basement. Dad did some cooking, but mostly he loved to bake. It was something he had learned from Grandma. Sometimes on a Saturday he would have us crowd into our little kitchen with him and we'd go crazy. Cakes, pies, cookies. Not too many at once of course, because there's always next week. Pies were Dad's specialty, and he was particular about the crust. He taught us to cut the shortening into the flour using two butter knives held together in one hand. At various times we made apple, peach, pumpkin, strawberry-rhubarb, lemon meringue, and banana cream. At Christmastime he made his traditional 'romance' cookies. He only made them once a year, so they were special and we all looked forward to them. They're a sweet, chewy coconut and walnut layer topped by a layer of shortbread. Many of his kids and grandkids have incorporated them into their own Christmas traditions. He also made delicious apple fritters and we sometimes had them for a quick Saturday supper. They were round balls of dough formed around chunks of sour apple, deep fried and sprinkled with powdered sugar. He served them with little slices of cheddar cheese 'to cut the sweetness.' They were so good!

For Dad, gardening was both satisfying and necessary. He had learned a great deal from his parents and he had a big garden that he tilled every year by hand. He planted some of his seeds inside very early in the spring. They would sit in the windows of the basement under special lights he had rigged up. He tended them carefully and as soon as the ground was warm enough, his little plants would be ready to be transplanted outside. He would come home from work and go out to water and weed the garden. He grew vegetables all summer and we'd have food all winter. We had fresh lettuce and radishes and peas and garlic. Zucchini, tomatoes, and cucumbers were plentiful. He would make sweet, tangy currant sauce to pour over rice, and pancake syrup from the pears on our tree. Delicious. And his berries! He had some blackberries and some raspberries, but the ones that commanded most of his attention were the strawberries. Dad grew the best strawberries, covering the runners with dirt every year to make new plants, and draping the bed with burlap in the fall to protect the plants from the harsh winter. He had several different varieties of strawberries. Some were for shortcake, some were for pies and some were for jam, which he and mom would often make together. He was very particular about which variety was used to make what. He and Mom made piccalilli too, diligently cutting and chopping the vegetables. He also grew rhubarb and blueberries. When the blueberries started to appear on the bushes, he would hang big blankets of cheesecloth over them so the birds couldn't help themselves. When it was time to pick, he would remove the cheesecloth, pick the berries that were ready and then cover them again. Gram would come over and help Mom can applesauce and spaghetti sauce and beans and peaches. I was terrified of the pressure cooker. I had heard stories about them blowing up and I would not go near the kitchen if one of those dreaded things was hissing on the stove. I was also keenly aware of the danger of a grease fire while cooking. I had seen one flare up one day while Mom was making dinner. It was small and quickly extinguished, but I reacted by running upstairs and slamming my bedroom door behind me.

Just like Grandma and Grandpa, Dad's gardens included colorful flowers and shrubs. He planted pink bleeding hearts next to the garage, red roses and sweet-smelling lavender-hued lilacs alongside our front steps. The bleeding hearts always intrigued me and sometimes I would pluck one off and stare at it, examining the odd-but-beautiful way it was shaped. Against the shady side of our house were white lily of the valley, tiny and delicate but incredibly fragrant. And in a flower garden in the back, just in front of the grape trellis, were irises and snapdragons in a variety of reds and blues and yellows. Climbing a small wire fence between our back yard and our neighbors' were purple morning glories. The fence wasn't very long and didn't seem to serve any purpose other than to give the vines a place to grow. I found the morning glories fascinating. There was just something about the way they climbed their way upward, reaching for the sun, that I found joyful.

***

Our father had some unusual ways to get us to comply with his wishes. Patty and I often could not go to sleep until long after our lights were turned out. We amused ourselves by playing word or memory games or just chatting. Sometimes it went on for a long time. Dad would yell up the stairs, "Go to sleep, you two!" One night, after we'd gone on talking and giggling for much too long, I heard a low growling noise coming from inside our room and said, "Patty, knock it off." "It wasn't me." "Of course it was you. It wasn't me, and we're the only ones here." Again, a deep growl. Now I was worried. "Patty, I said knock it off." Before she could respond, it happened for the third time, and Patty got scared. "Carol, stop it! It's not funny." We both became quiet, listening but hearing nothing more. Suddenly Dad stood up in the middle of our room, between our two beds, and said, "Now be quiet and go to sleep." Then he walked out. He had silently crawled into our room on his hands and knees and we had been so busy chattering away that we had not heard him.

When I was a little older and decided I'd rather just stay in bed than get up for school, he had remedies for that too. First, he would come in and call me. When he got no response, he'd start flicking the light switch. On, off, on, off, on, off. It drove me nuts. I got up. After a few times I realized I could simply pull the covers over my head and not be bothered by the flicking of the lights. Not to be outdone, Dad devised another strategy. He stood at the foot of my bed and, with his knees, he gave the bed a nudge. Then another, and another. "Oh, for crying out loud! All right, I'll get up!"

He also had his own brand of discipline. If I did something deserving of punishment, he could make me feel just awful. He would take me upstairs and sit me on the bed, away from the prying ears of my siblings, and talk to me in a way that would make me wish he would just hit me and get it over with. But, of course, he would never hit anyone. He was always so good, so right, so fair that it upset me to know he was disappointed in me. When I was seventeen, I had a terrible fight with my mother. I don't even remember what it was about. I had met a boy at camp that summer who lived with his dad in New York City and we sometimes talked on the phone, so I decided to run away from home and call Danny to come and get me. What I did was pretty brave for a small-town girl who had never gone anywhere on her own. Or maybe it was just stupid. I got a ride to Albany, bought a bus ticket with my baby-sitting money and went off to New York. Once there, I was amazed at how loud and crowded and frantic it was. I had no money, didn't know anyone, probably looked scared, surely looked alone. I called Danny. He came for me and took me to his father's house. I don't know what my next step would have been; I didn't have a plan beyond running away. But Danny's father called my dad and put me on the next bus back to Albany. Dad met me at the bus station and drove me home in silence. Back at our house, he took me upstairs. "Oh god," I thought. "Here we go." But this time he didn't talk about the trouble I'd caused. Instead, he told me how incredibly worried he'd been and how much danger I had put myself in. When he was finished and walking out of the room, I had the audacity to ask him if he'd drive me to go roller skating with my friends. I will never forget his response; it was so typical of him. "Under the circumstances, I don't think I'm inclined to oblige."

Dad still worked as a stenographer for Gulf Oil Corporation, a job he had originally taken when he was first assigned to reserve duty in 1946. Over the years, his active duty stints often had to be charged to vacation time at Gulf Oil and that didn't make

Mom very happy. If it was summertime and they didn't send him too far away, he would sometimes take the family with him. We would stay at a campsite, he would join us at night, and we'd call it a vacation. I know at least twice our two weeks were spent in Plattsburgh, NY – about 160 miles from home. Mom often voiced her displeasure with Gulf for not honoring Dad's service by giving him the two weeks for active duty without making him forfeit the time for a real vacation – one where we could swim and Dad could be with us all day. The job he had was far from what he had envisioned doing with his life, but he had to support his family. He never had the chance to go to college, although he could have aced any subject he chose to pursue. In his youth, he had all the makings of a superstar. Instead, his marriage to my mother at a very young age stalled, and ultimately put an end to, his military career. But through all the disappointment he must have felt, despite all the unfulfilled dreams and unmet expectations, he was always a kind, thoughtful, loving man.

***

The only vacations we took were in a beat-up old camping trailer that Dad bought second-hand. When he first got it, he pulled it with his big old Mercury. The paint on the car was two-tone, a popular trend at the time. It was blue-green and off-white, very pretty, and the car was a rare splurge he had allowed himself. The outside of the trailer was a mess, so what did Dad do? Well, he painted it the same colors as the car, of course. I'm sure it amused many people as we drove by them on the highway. At first, he pulled it around to different campgrounds during the summer and stored it in our back yard during the winter. Once, on our way to somewhere, Dad had stopped at a traffic light that was at the bottom of a steep hill, the trailer behind us. As we sat there, we felt and heard a violent thump. Dad got out of the car to investigate. Someone with bad brakes had come down the hill behind us and had plowed right through the back wall of our trailer. I don't recall how that got fixed, but we must have turned around and gone back home. After a few years, when the trailer became in danger of falling apart, Dad rented a year-round site on a beautiful lake in the Adirondacks and there it stayed for many years. We enjoyed it so much! Dad reinforced the structure, built bunkbeds in the back bedroom to accommodate more of us and attached a large screened-in porch where my brother often slept and where we would play cards and board games on rainy days.

Dad loved making breakfast at camp. Whenever possible he would build a fire and cook outside, often using his favorite old cast iron skillets – bacon in one, pancakes in the other. He swore pancakes tasted best when cooked on cast iron. He was very particular, waiting until the outside edge of the pancake started to firm up and the center was full of bubbles. Only then would he flip it to cook the other side. Yum!

We needed milk one day and Mom asked me to walk to the store to get some. The store she was talking about was a small place, catering mostly to campers and offering the things they were likely to run out of. I knew the owner well; his son was a good friend of mine. She handed me some money and off I went. My friend's dad smiled at me and said hello as I walked in. He was very nice and I liked him a lot. I grabbed the milk, went to the counter, and handed him the ten dollar bill my mother had given me. He slid some change across the counter and I balled it up in the palm of my hand so I wouldn't lose it, carrying the milk in my other hand. When I got back to our campsite, Mom and Dad were both inside the trailer. I passed the milk to Mom, opened my other hand, let the coins fall onto the counter and began to smooth out the bills so I could hand them to her. "Oh no," I said, "I have to go back. He gave me too much money." There was a ten where a single should have been. "No," was Mom's immediate response, "we can use…" "Shirley," Dad said quietly, looking directly at her. Then he turned to me. "Carol, take it all back so he can see what he did, then let him give you the correct change." I learned something that day. Passively acquiring a little badly-needed money and wanting to keep it is probably a forgivable offense. But my father's firm decision to return it was the better choice. If it isn't yours, it isn't yours. Period.

We hiked and swam and sat by campfires every night, roasting marshmallows or making popcorn. I took long, long walks, usually by myself. We were very close to a public, state-operated campground, so I often walked through the gate and all around the winding dirt roads, humming to myself and absentmindedly looking at the huge variety of tents and trailers as I passed by. On rainy days, Monopoly, Canasta, and Scrabble would keep us occupied for hours. Dad bought himself a 'Sailfish', a small sailboat that was really just an overgrown surfboard with a sail attached. He had a lot of fun on it, but I don't recall any of us kids being interested in it. Dad used to be fond of saying, "We don't have a lot of money but we have a lot of fun."

One summer, my brother found a way to frighten all of us with his curiosity. Brandon was off our campsite, but well within sight, where there was a large boulder in a common area and lots of people were milling around. He was pounding on the boulder with a smaller rock. From where I stood it looked like he was trying to smash something. I glanced at Dad. "What's Brandon doing over there?" He walked over to investigate. When he came back, he said nonchalantly, "He found an old spent rifle shell. It's ok." The second those words left his mouth, we heard a loud noise and then a high-pitched whistling sound. Dad turned white. The damn thing had been live, and Brandon had managed to ignite the gunpowder. The bullet was gone, but we never knew which direction it had shot off in or where it ended up. Somebody could have been seriously injured that day!

Many of my favorite summer days were spent on water skis. My parents had friends in western New York with a son my age and a beautiful boat. Craig and his Dad taught me to waterski when I was eleven. I got up successfully the first time and absolutely loved it. Crossing the wake, starting either in deep water or off the dock, learning to drop one ski – it all seemed pretty easy to me. I guess if you're young and strong, you can do almost anything. When I was seventeen, Craig and his family came to our camp for a visit. We had skied together quite a bit over the years and, of course, they brought their boat. We were out on the water a lot that day and then decided to try something. The boat had plenty of power to pull both of us at the same time. Craig usually skied on his right leg and I skied on my left, so we started out with each of us on two skis, me to his right. With Craig's father operating the boat, after we were both up out of the water, Craig dropped his left ski. Then, instead of planting his left leg on the back of his remaining ski, he kept it hanging over the water. I swooped in close to him and dropped my left ski, stepping over and planting my dominant leg on the back of his ski. Then, when I had my balance, I dropped my right ski. Now we were both on the same single ski! We didn't get very far that way, but it sure was fun trying. Dad wasn't in the boat; for some reason he wasn't all that fond of motor boats. But he was up on the dock watching us, shaking his head in amusement and disbelief.

I made of lot of friends at camp and quite a few of them had access to family boats. I considered myself lucky to have many opportunities to be out on the water. I was old enough to go off on my own, so I often skied with my friends. One day when I was riding along comfortably on two skis, I found myself with too much slack in the towrope. I started to fall and somehow, in trying to regain my balance, the handle of the rope went between my knees. As I crashed into the water, the rope wound around my thigh just as there was immediate tension on it from the pull of my body being drug through the water. Now there were two problems. First, unless you can free yourself of the rope, as long as the boat keeps pulling you, you are somehow forced down farther and farther under the water. I don't understand the science of it, but it does not allow you to stay up near the surface. Second, at that moment my friends were breaking the cardinal rule of waterskiing: the spotters in the boat never, ever take their eyes off the skier. I was fighting with every ounce of strength I had but I could not free myself of the rope. Just as my lungs were about to burst and I was sure I was going to pass out and drown, the driver of the boat felt the drag and turned to look at me. When he saw I wasn't there, he cut the motor. As soon as he did that, I rose quickly to the surface and immediately started gasping for air. I had a nasty rope burn around my thigh. When I walked back into camp my mother saw it and asked me what happened. As I started to explain, Dad came over. I was visibly shaken as I told my story and he put his hand on my shoulder. "Carol," he said, "here's what I think you should do. Unless you want to be terrified of water skiing for the rest of your life, I think you should take a few minutes to calm down and then go right back out there. And this time, make sure you can trust the people you choose to go out with." I took his advice.

I don't know how many years that old trailer was in our family. We certainly used it up and wore it out. Years later, after Dad died, it fell upon me to clean out his house and get things ready for the others to come and claim what they wanted. My hands touched every single item and piece of paper he had owned, and I created spreadsheets to keep track of all of it. He'd been such a pack-rat, never able to throw anything away. The basement was chock-full of useless old stuff. There was a big, heavy safe containing years and years of old tax returns and ancient bank statements and checkbook registers. There were dozens of jars they had used for canning the bounty from Dad's gardens. The jars were ok, but the metal tops were all rusted. There were pieces of lumber and leftover wallpaper, now torn and faded. From nails pounded into the rafters hung plastic shopping bags with all sorts of odds and ends that he thought he might use some day, and there were coffee cans and mayonnaise jars filled with mismatched nails and screws and washers and bolts. Need an old doorknob? He had that. A roll of rusty chicken wire? Yup. The garage was just as bad. One day as I was dragging archaic bedframes and storm windows down out of the rafters in the garage, I spotted some old painted cabinets. "Where did those come from?" I wondered. As I pulled them out of their hiding space, they started to look familiar. Then I laughed. They were out of the old camping trailer. The rest of the trailer had been trashed years before but hey, you never know when you might need some crummy old cabinets out of a beat-up old trailer.

***

Dad played accordion and I would often sit on the floor at his feet and stare at his fingers while he played. How did his left hand know which buttons to push when he couldn't even see them? I was intrigued. When I was eleven, he agreed to let me take lessons, even though he and Mom really had no money to spare. He asked the band director at our school if he knew anyone who taught accordion. That's where he got Joe's name. I started learning on Dad's old accordion, a small one with 24 bass buttons. Once a week after school I had to take the bus, schlepping that big heavy instrument, and go into Albany for my lesson. Then Dad would leave his office, which was about ten minutes away, to pick me up and drive me home. After a couple of years Dad somehow managed to surprise me with a brand-new accordion of my own – one with 120 bass buttons. It was beautiful and made for a woman's hands, with keys that were just slightly smaller than those on a standard size accordion. At Dad's request, my teacher had gone to the factory and picked it out himself. Now that there were two accordions in the house, we would take them with us to camp and play together outside by the campfire. Often, people from neighboring campsites would come to listen.

Joe was a good teacher and I liked him because he played accordion like nobody I'd ever seen. In my opinion, he was every bit as good as Myron Floren on the Lawrence Welk Show. He was also an incredible piano player, and playing at clubs and for private events was the main source of his income. He taught me in his living room and although his wife had introduced herself to me once, I almost never saw her. He also had two kids, a daughter just slightly older than me and a boy a couple of years younger. He mentioned them a couple of times, but I don't believe I ever met them. They probably couldn't stand listening to their father's students playing in the living room. Once in a while Joe would play a song for me, either on the piano or the accordion, just to entertain me. He had perfect pitch and we'd play a game where I would roll my fists around on his piano and then hit a single note. Without looking, he named the note correctly every single time. He said I could learn to do it too, that learning to identify and name pitches was the same as learning to identify and name colors. I never proved or disproved his theory, because I wasn't interested enough to really try.

I already knew how to read music, I had learned that in school, but he taught me how to put notes together to form chords. Major, minor, sixth, seventh, diminished. And he taught me how to maneuver my way around the bass buttons to take full advantage of them. Each week we'd choose a song for me to learn and most of the time he would sit with blank staff paper and write an arrangement for me by hand as he whistled the melody to himself. It was impressive to watch him. I still have several spiral books full of his hand-written music. Sometimes he'd ask me to transpose what he had written into a different key when I got home and then learn to play it in the new key for him when I returned the following week. He had me purchase the sheet music for a few difficult classics. "Flight of the Bumblebee," "The Jolly Caballero," an incredibly complicated version of "Tea for Two." I loved the intricacies of those pieces and my fingers flew over the keys once I mastered them. Joe was a good teacher and I became a pretty accomplished musician. I played in a few local shows and was hired for a couple of wedding receptions while still in high school, and when I was accepted to play in a talent show on a local TV station, Dad drove me to the studio and watched proudly while we taped the show. I mostly played accordion but Joe insisted on teaching me some piano too, because he thought my left hand should be trained to play piano keys as well as the accordion bass buttons.

After studying with him for several years, Joe did something that made me very uncomfortable. I always sat on the piano bench with my back to the piano and my accordion resting on my legs as I played. Joe always sat in a chair facing me. One day, as I was in the middle of a song, he leaned toward me and slid a hand between the accordion and my body, and then down between my legs. Then he just left it there. I was fourteen years old and I didn't know what to do. Nothing like this had ever happened before. I ignored him, sat as still as possible, and went on playing. The following week the same thing happened. By the third week, as he started to reach over, I mustered up all my courage, stopped playing, looked at the floor and said quietly, "Stop." He did. After that he kept his hand to himself and we both acted as if it had never happened. I never told anyone. My father really liked Joe and I was sure he wouldn't believe me.

Joe had another student who called himself 'Spike'. He was a year older than me, Italian and gorgeous. I had such a crush on him! He lived in Albany and his lesson was often just before mine. Because I took the bus to get there, I was sometimes a bit early, and I was always invited to sit quietly and listen. We got to know each other a little and couldn't help flirting. I was scheduled to appear on a community show put on by the Kiwanis in my hometown and held in the auditorium of my high school. Spike and I were both accomplished players and Joe had an idea. The night of the show, when it was my turn to perform, I took the stage and played one song. Then I introduced Spike and he joined me on stage. We started the piece together, but in the middle of the number, still playing, I turned my back to the audience so the keyboard on my accordion was nearly touching the keyboard on Spike's accordion. Without missing a beat, I reached over to his keyboard, he reached over to mine and we finished the song, arms crossed. I was playing my bass buttons and his keyboard, he was playing his bass buttons and my keyboard. The audience loved it.

My accordion was my most cherished possession. I learned how to take the front panel off and expose the reeds because once in a while a little dust would get in one of them and I would have to blow it out. Then one of the bass notes started sticking so I took off that cover panel and figured out what was wrong. I cleaned and polished it regularly and took really good care of it. One day in the future I would be able to return Dad's thoughtfulness by buying him a new accordion. His beat-up old squeezebox was shot. The new one had 120 bass buttons, just like mine. He never learned how to use most of them, but it made him happy just the same. I reclaimed it after he died, but I recently sold it in a garage sale. It had been in my closet for fifteen years and it was time for it to be played again. Although I don't take it out much anymore, I still have the one he bought for me and I have very fond memories of when we played together. "The Blue Skirt Waltz." "Beer Barrell Polka." "Red Sails in the Sunset." Those songs and others can all make me feel both happy and melancholy.

I sang in the school choir, as well as select choir. Patty played trombone in the school band, as well as dance band. We loved to play together. After school, we would sit on our beds and play for hours. Practicing was never work for us, because we had so much fun. I can't even describe how much enjoyment we derived over the years from our wonderful shared hobby. Because her trombone was a B-flat instrument, if she wanted to play some of my written music with me, I had to transpose it by hand onto blank staff paper for her to use. I got lots of practice doing that! Over time she became a much better musician than I. She played in dance bands and German oompah bands and orchestras. Patty mastered all the brass instruments and was equally comfortable picking up her trombone, a trumpet, a tuba or a euphonium. She could sight-read with incredible speed and accuracy. That amazed me.

One summer, when Patty was playing with a German band, she somehow talked the other members into coming up to our camp. They all showed up in the morning with their bathing suits and food to share. Some of them went down to the beach, others hung out at the dock. It was a beautiful day and, after enjoying the water for a couple of hours, they came back to camp and we had a delicious pot luck cook-out. When everything was cleaned up, they set up their music stands alongside our trailer. The stands were decorated with the band's logo, just as if they were playing in a show or at an Octoberfest, and it all looked very impressive. They took turns using the back bedroom of the trailer to change into their lederhosen and then they let 'er rip! They were really good and they were really loud, and curious people started showing up from campsites all around. My sister was clearly having a blast, and

Dad was in seventh heaven! He was so supportive of us, and always encouraged our artistic endeavors. Much later in my life, when I began singing and competing in a cappella quartets, he would come to various shows to watch me perform and blow me kisses from his seat in the audience as I stood in front of the mic.

***

I'm sure Dad's favorite time of the year was Christmas. On Christmas Eve he would take us to Candlelight Service at our church. I loved the music and the intimacy of the sanctuary as each of us held a lit candle and the electric lights were turned off one by one. I loved the telling of the Christmas story and the excitement of the children who tried to sit still while anticipating the visitor who would be coming down their chimneys later that night. Outside of church Dad delighted in Christmas carols and holiday songs. I can't even begin to imagine how many renditions of "Jolly Old Saint Nicholas" he sang, while accompanying himself on the accordion. He loved Santa Clauses of all kinds. He drew them. He cut them out of wood. He once made a life-sized Santa with his jigsaw, complete with Rudolph and a sleigh, painted them and put them on our roof. Santa had a big white overstuffed bag slung over his shoulder and rosy red cheeks. He was winking. They were all lit up and very festive. As a matter of fact, our whole street was festive! Everybody wanted to have the best, the biggest, the brightest Christmas display on the block. It was a competition of sorts and it was so much fun driving around the roads at night to see what everyone else had done. Our tree was often put up and decorated on Christmas Eve, each of us participating according to our age and ability. Dad was very particular about Christmas trees. When everything was done except for the tinsel, he took over. Only he applied the tinsel, one single strand at a time starting at the bottom and working up to the top. It was painstakingly slow and we soon lost interest. But he persisted until the task was completed and the tree was perfect. Now, I hang the tinsel every year. I don't enjoy the job as much as he seemed to, but Christmas just wouldn't be the same without tinsel on the tree, so I carry on the tradition.

Our parents scrimped and saved all year so we would have a wonderful Christmas. Dad said he wanted to make sure that our Christmases weren't like his when he wished and wished for something that Santa never brought. He once told me that he and his brothers would feel lucky and grateful to get nothing but a fresh orange in their stockings, because fresh citrus fruit was unheard of in the wintertime when he was a kid. Patty and I liked to watch the Howdy Doody show, so one Christmas Santa brought us marionettes. One of us got Howdy and the other got Mr. Bluster. With the strings, we could control their arms and legs and move their heads and open their mouths. Sometimes we put on little shows, pretending we were on TV and trying to make our voices sound authentic. We loved them, but did they ever get tangled! Any time we put them down the strings got all twisted and wrapped around each other. Dad was the most patient person I ever knew. Over and over, with great diligence, he would unravel the messes we had made of them. When Patty and I no longer played with them, two of our sisters claimed them for themselves. I think they still have them.

I loved all the smells of Christmas. Turkey roasting in the oven, evergreen trees, cinnamon, cloves, fresh-baked sugar cookies and gingerbread men. What a wonderful time of the year! It was a time of excitement and anticipation and a time for visiting relatives. Over the course of a few days we would go to see each aunt and uncle, grandmother and grandfather, and they would come to visit us. Except for Dad's two brothers, of course. We never went to their houses and they never came to ours. At each stop, we would look forward to some beautifully decorated cookies or maybe some eggnog. Then everyone who lived in the house would take a turn sitting under the tree and showing each present he or she had received. Someone would always remark on the beauty of the Christmas tree and ask about the origins of various ornaments, even if we'd heard it a hundred times before. Grandma's Christmas trees were always awesome to me because they looked so different from the trees we had in our house during the holidays. Hers were decorated with old, fragile ornaments that she'd been using since Dad was a little boy. I would stand by the tree, examining each one. We were allowed to touch them, but ever so gently. Sometimes now I'll see old Christmas tree decorations in an antique store and find one or two that look exactly like the ones I remember on Grandma's tree.

***

Dad drew and painted other things besides Santas. Watercolor still-lifes, adobe buildings he'd seen in Texas, an oil painting of a winter scene featuring a very large bunny, a charcoal sketch of a couple in old-fashioned garb, ice skating hand-in-hand. Dad once told me he'd first noticed Mom while ice skating, and the woman in the sketch looks like Mom. And pink – he used a lot of pink in flowers, in sunsets. One of my sisters lives in California, and for a couple of years after he died, we used to call each other if one of us was looking at a particularly pink sunset and say, "Dad's painting the sky tonight." I have some of his artwork. He very seldom framed anything he did, but I framed them and have them proudly displayed throughout my home.

He also had a real eye for decorating, and loved perking up a tired old room with a fresh coat of paint, a lamp moved to just the right spot or perhaps new window shades or curtains to replace old, shabby ones. I was very interested in why he chose certain colors for certain spaces, why asymmetry is sometimes the best way to balance a room, and how you can make things more interesting by mixing textures. I soon found out that my taste was very much like his, and to this day I don't like anything too fussy; clean lines and simple, uncluttered patterns were his style, and mine too. He would ask me for my opinion when he was choosing paint or rearranging furniture and he always made me feel that he factored my suggestions into his decisions. He enjoyed hanging wallpaper, and once I was out on my own, so did I. But it was easier for me; when Dad was doing it, wallpaper wasn't pre-pasted. He'd set up workhorses with a long board across the top where he could roll out the paper, cut it to just the right size and brush on the thick, sticky paste with a big, wide brush. I loved watching him, and the result was always perfect when he got done, the patterns being matched up just so. Once, when he decided that the room Patty and I shared needed some updating, he brought home a book of wallpaper samples and thrilled me by allowing me to pick out the pattern. Then he did his magic, and voila! A fresh, new room. I remember the satisfied feeling I had for weeks, every time I went upstairs. It's amazing what an impact a simple thing like wallpaper can have on your outlook.

In addition to our shared interests in music, baking, and home decorating, Dad and I had many other things in common. We both loved to read and we were both good with numbers and problem-solving. Surely, I told myself, I had gotten my intelligence from him. And I believed I had been blessed with his temperament, although I wasn't sure you could inherit something like that. Over time, I developed my patience and the ability to let many things 'roll off my back' by modeling myself after him. He taught me to be resourceful, confident, trustworthy and polite. And we both had good organizational skills. To this day, I keep notes and schedules and to-do lists, just like he did. Mom was quite short, but my brother and I were both tall like Dad. She had green eyes, but all of us kids had blue eyes like his. There were so many things about him that I loved, and so many reasons why I always felt proud, grateful, and happy to be my father's daughter.

It was hard growing up feeling stuck between a dad who was wonderful in so many ways and a mom who was so often impossible to like or respect. Dad continued in the reserves, doing occasional two-week active duty tours. On 1/4/1957 he was promoted to Major. In April of '61 they welcomed daughter number four and in July of '63, their last baby was born. My brother, who had just turned ten, informed Dad that if Mom came home with another girl he was going to run away. She did. He didn't. There are sixteen years between me and my youngest sister. Among the six of us, the differences in our personalities and the spread of our ages meant we all had slightly different experiences with our mother. She wasn't physically disabled when I was growing up, but a few years after the birth of her last child she was diagnosed with multiple sclerosis and some of the younger ones had to deal with the progression of her disease, in addition to her disagreeable personality. We all coped in different ways and some remain more affected than others. I hope they find a way to heal.

***

Finally, on December 16, 1965 – six months after I graduated from high school, and three months after I got married and moved out of the house – Dad was promoted to Lieutenant Colonel. I have a copy of a 'training report' from the 9261st Air Reserve Squadron in Albany that says in part, "Lt. Col. Jones* has proven to be an invaluable asset to the Reserve Program. He displays much initiative, is highly competent and can be depended on to carry out assignments without supervision. He is neat and well groomed. A likeable officer who has the unique personality of being able to get along with all his colleagues. His cooperativeness and loyalty to the Reserve program make him a credit to the Air Force Reserve." A few months later, at his request, he was placed on the Reserve Retired list and relieved from assignment. He was only forty years old.

*our family name has been changed

Dad was the highest-ranking service man in our village and each year, at the end of the ceremony that followed the Memorial Day Parade, he would lead the 21-gun salute over our local cemetery. One year, as I stood next to him, listening to the speakers on the podium, I looked up and said, "Dad, I'm so proud of you." He was seldom emotional, but that brought a tear to his eye and he responded simply and quietly, "Thank you." It made me happy to see that my words had touched him. He was occasionally asked to speak to groups of school children, usually at an assembly during Veterans' Day or Memorial Day. He would talk about the war and his experiences in the service. He would show them pictures of 'his' B-29 and Quonset huts and bomb damage. He talked about how they used radar, which was brand new when he first got his training. I have a hand-written note that he must have used for one of his presentations. It says, "Tomorrow, Oct 28th is 'Make a Difference Day' which stresses the importance of community service. Each of you owes some form of community service when you reach young adulthood." I had to look up 'Make a Difference Day' and was surprised to find that it is a real 'thing' and it is still observed. According to one website it is one of the largest annual single-day service events nationwide. Thousands of volunteers across the country unite on the fourth Saturday in October, with the common mission of improving the lives of others through a wide range of community-based service projects. Dad was teaching those kids the same values he had tried to instill in us.

His own community service had included being a volunteer fireman. The fire siren could be heard all over town, blasting out a code. He would drop whatever he was doing and run to the kitchen to look at the chart that hung on the wall. Finding the code on the chart, he could tell where in town the fire was and he would be out of the house and off in a flash to do his part. I don't think any of us kids thought much about it; it was just something he did. But I once asked him if he was ever scared or felt he was in danger. He said there was only one fire that had been so large, so intense, that he thought he or someone else might die. Imagining that sent a chill through me.

CHAPTER EIGHT

I should have learned from Dad's mistakes. I should have taken some time, figured out what I wanted out of life. I should have trusted my abilities and ventured out on my own, exploring, trying new things, until I found what was right for me. But I didn't. I took what seemed like the easy way out and opted for marriage. I had been eighteen, just out of high school. One of the last things I did before graduating was to take an entry-level state exam in the hope of getting employment with New York State. Then I agreed to accept a summer job at a local snack bar while waiting for a job offer from the state to come in the mail. The owners lived in our village and knew my parents. I met Don at the snack bar, where he came and sat for several hours a day, every day, shooting the breeze with the owners, the 'regulars' and friends of his who would drop by on the weekends. He was twenty-seven, out of work ('laid off' from his construction job, he said) and living with his mother and step-father. I had two uncles who did construction work and I knew they occasionally got laid off, so it didn't seem odd to me, even though it was summertime. He seemed nice and was fun to talk to and I liked his friends so, although he was nine years older than me, I agreed to go out with him. He took me to a local bar with live music where I was surprised to find out he was a good dancer. We enjoyed a few of those kinds of dates, usually with another couple. He drove a Corvette hard-top convertible, something I had never seen before, and I was fascinated by the process of removing the top and putting it back on. You might wonder how a man who wasn't working could be driving a car like that. I wondered too. So, I asked.

When he was eight years old, Don and his father were crossing a street on foot, hand-in-hand. They were both hit by a car. His father was killed instantly, and Don was in a coma for eight days with extensive injuries. There was a lawsuit and a substantial settlement, which was held in trust for Don until he turned twenty-one. As soon as he collected, he began to spend. He was now twenty-seven, and the purchase of the Corvette a year ago had been his last gasp. He had blown through all of it. Over the course of five years, he had owned four sports cars – all brand new. What he didn't spend on cars, he had used to buy expensive stereo equipment, gold jewelry for himself, and diamond bracelets for a girlfriend who left him when the money ran out. His mother had remarried and he continued to live in her house, no contribution toward rent or utilities required – she was just grateful that he was alive. But now his bank account was wiped out and he was broke. My timing has always been lousy.

Within weeks, the first of my awaited job offers came. It was in New York City. That was unexpected because most New York State jobs are in the capital city of Albany, but I was excited at the prospect. Dad cautioned me to be careful and to weigh all the pros and cons before agreeing to an interview. I could tell he didn't like the idea of me going to New York, and frankly, I was a little nervous, but I decided to go anyhow. When I walked into the expansive lobby of a big building in Manhattan, I was very impressed. There were tall columns, marble walls, unimaginably high ceilings and a massive staircase. I stopped at the visitors' desk, found out where I needed to go and took the elevator upstairs to meet the man who was to interview me. I liked him, I liked what he had to say about the job, and he liked me. I had gotten a very high mark on the exam and was just the kind of person they were looking for. With one exception.

"Where are you from?" he queried.

"A small village outside of Albany. I'm sure you've never heard of it."

"Who do you know in New York City?"

"Nobody."

"If I hire you, where will you live?"

"I don't know. I thought I could stay at the 'Y' until I have enough money to get an apartment."

"I have a daughter about your age. May I speak to you as a parent?"

"Sure."

"I fear this city would swallow you up before you could blink an eye. You're going to get lots more job offers from this exam list and most of them will be in Albany. Go home and wait for one of those. You're a smart, likeable girl with a bright future but I cannot in good conscience ask you to move down here with absolutely no support system in place. Thank you for coming, be safe getting home and I wish you nothing but the best."

I have to say, I was both a little disappointed and a little relieved.

Don took me to his mother's house one day because he needed to pick something up. The house was a duplex; they lived on one side and there were tenants on the other side. I knew his parents weren't home; in the summer they stayed in Rhode Island. He told me to wait in the car, but I followed him in anyhow. Holy crap! The place was disgusting! He hadn't done dishes in a month, at least. The sink was completely filled with unwashed plates and cups and glasses and silverware. There were smelly clothes everywhere and every pot and pan in the place was dirty. Some contained rotting, moldy food, and they were sitting all over the stove and the kitchen table. The floors were filthy and there was no empty space on any of the furniture to sit down. He was clearly embarrassed but he laughed it off and said that every year he cleaned it up before they came back home. "How can you possibly clean this up?" I asked. "Easy, I throw everything out and buy new stuff." "The dishes, the pots and pans, the clothes?" "Everything."

We took a ride to his parents' summer home in Rhode Island where I met his very Italian family, who lived an extremely loud, boisterous life unlike anything I'd experienced before. It seemed very chaotic to me, but I guess it was really just different from what I was used to. They had a big old sprawling home, right on the ocean, and I could not have walked into a world more different from the one I had always known. They yelled and argued all the time and called each other names, but were never really angry. For them, a meal wasn't complete without the accompanying disagreements and bickering. I quickly learned what all the Italian curse words were, which ones were mild and which ones were awful. It was strange and at times unsettling, and I didn't always know how to react, but they were very nice to me and his mother kept telling me, "You the best-a thing that ever happened to my Donnie." We ate a lot of food and drank a lot of coffee. I didn't even like coffee, but it was a social thing in his family; people always talked over a cup of coffee. We went clamming and deep-sea fishing. Two-and-a-half months after graduating from high school I married him – not because I loved him, but because it seemed like an ok alternative to remaining in my parents' house, and because he told me his heart had been broken once before and if I broke it again, he would kill himself.

Of course, we had to be married in the Catholic Church, even though Don never went to church. It was the rule, apparently. Our wedding reception was in the local VFW hall where Dad was a member. Relatives on both sides supplied the food, and for our wedding toast we drank some god-awful home-made Italian wine made by Don's stepfather. Our honeymoon was a two-day trip to Niagara Falls, including a quick visit to the Canadian side. After the first day, Don seemed a little distracted and edgy, and already I had a vague, nagging feeling that I was taking my life in the wrong direction. But I stubbornly ignored it because I didn't have a better idea.

I got to work learning how to be a good Italian wife. My mother-in-law had said to me, "If-a you gonna marry my Donnie, you got-a learn to cook Italian. An' you got-a have a nice-a hot meal on-a the table when he get home from work." Pasta was on the menu every Sunday and every Thursday, no exceptions. She taught me to make sauce the 'right' way – with pork, beef, meatballs and chicken all simmering in the pot. We made homemade Italian bread, homemade sausage – stuffed by hand using a funnel, homemade pasta – hung over the backs of the dishtowel-draped kitchen chairs. Then we moved on to ravioli, rolling out the dough as thin as possible, cutting it into squares and filling each one with a mixture of ricotta cheese, eggs, garlic, parsley and grated parmesan and sealing the edges with the tines of a fork. Those were my favorites; they were quite tasty. And with homemade braciole to go with them – delizioso! We made ricotta pie for Easter and deep-fried Italian cookies, sprinkled with powdered sugar, at Christmastime. With the best of intentions, my mother-in-law offered words of wisdom. "Wherever he goes, you go. Wherever you go, he goes." "He's your husband. He's the boss." And this gem: "It's woman's lot in life to take whatever her husband gives her." I was never really sure what that one meant; it can be taken several different ways and I didn't like any of them. But I learned to cater to him, wait on him, take care of him.

My in-laws had some strange customs that took me by surprise, to say the least. One morning, we were sitting at the kitchen table having coffee when my mother-in-law looked at me and began to burp. She announced, "Somebody give-a you the maloik."

"Maloik?" I asked. Don started to laugh. "The evil eye. Ma thinks somebody gave you the evil eye." She got up and poured a little water into a bowl. Then she put a few drops of olive oil in the bowl and held the bowl over my head, moving it in slow circles. What the....? She lowered the bowl and peered into it. The oil had made little snake-like shapes on the water, like thick pieces of floating thread. "It was a man!" she declared. She believed the ritual had cured me of the maloik. And I learned that if the oil had stayed in little round droplets, it would have indicated I'd been given the evil eye by a woman. I suspected the shape of the oil droplets had more to do with the temperature of the water, but I didn't dare say so. I saw that ritual performed many times, on many different family members. I guess there was no end to people giving each other the evil eye!

They also kept lists of things other people had done so, when the time came, they could respond in kind. The oddest list to me had two columns, labeled 'real' and 'fake'. Under each column heading were many names. I was told that each time there was a death in the family, they kept track of who sent real flowers and who sent fake flowers so they could return the favor by doing the same. After all, you wouldn't want to waste money on real flowers for a family that had given you fake ones. Kept in an envelope along with that list was a small collection of photographs. They were all pictures of dead babies, dressed in beautiful gowns, reposing in their tiny caskets. I don't know whose babies they were, and I don't know if this was a customary thing in Italian families or just a way to remember what the children looked like. I didn't ask. I thought it was creepy.

It didn't take long for me to learn just how needy and incompetent and dependent on his mother Don really was. He was either incapable of taking care of himself or just unwilling to bother. He handed me a shoe box full of bills, at least a year's worth, that he had forgotten to pay, didn't intend to pay or had to pay immediately because something was about to be repossessed. There was no order to any of the papers I found in the box. Many were from the same creditor, month after month, some opened, some not. Some had been crumpled up, but then put in the box anyhow. Some were covered in coffee stains or had pieces missing. There were letters from collection agencies and threats of garnished wages. I took care of them all – put them in order, called creditors, made deals. I became his secretary, his bookkeeper, his mother.

My next job offer came from New York State, this time in Albany, and after a successful interview, I gratefully accepted. I had taken driver's ed in school, but still hadn't gotten my driver's license, so every day my husband drove me to work in the morning, went back home to do nothing useful, and picked me up at 5:00. He sold the Corvette and replaced it with something more practical and I took my driving test so I could get myself back and forth to work. We bought a mobile home and his parents held the mortgage, but they foreclosed on it a year later because we couldn't pay for it. By now we had a daughter and we moved into the other half of his parents' duplex.

I was becoming acutely aware of a side of Don he hadn't shown me before we were married. He had a very short fuse and a terrible temper. He had a big, loud, booming voice and he raised it on a regular basis. He never hit me, but I was sometimes afraid of him and he often made me very upset. His personality was in stark contrast to my father who was always calm and thoughtful and temperate. When Don worked, it was usually with a road construction company. Sometimes he would operate heavy equipment, sometimes he would do other things, but he had a pattern worked out: Work the minimum required number of days, get laid off, collect unemployment. When the unemployment ran out, apply for an extension. When the extension ran out, go back to work for the required minimum number of days and begin the cycle again. I was twenty now and left my job because I could not find anyone I trusted to take care of my daughter. She was a beautiful little girl, sweet, bright, and funny. I loved being with her, teaching her, reading to her. When we were living in the mobile home, she spent the time I was at work with a trusted friend in a neighboring trailer. But now that we were living in my mother-in-law's house, that friend was too far away. Staying home made me happy, but it made our financial situation nearly impossible. Once, as I watched impatiently for one of Don's unemployment checks to come in the mail, I kept asking him to call and find out what was holding it up, but he would not do it. "Don, we need the money! It should be here by now. Please call!" As I pressed him on it, he blew his top and finally admitted there was no money coming, because when he'd checked in with the unemployment office, something he was periodically required to do, an employee there insisted he show proof that he was looking for a job. Of course, he had no proof because he hadn't been looking, and he told her to go fuck herself. I cried. I didn't know what else to do.

My husband's temper seemed to get worse as time went on. He had no patience with the kids and would often storm out of the house, slamming the door behind him. When he found that a tire on his car had gone flat, he kicked a big dent in the back fender with his work boot. If a toy was left in the driveway and he had to move it to get into the garage, he would pick it up and fling it across the yard. When the television wouldn't work, he grabbed the nearest available object and broke it over the TV. He once even picked up his own guitar and smashed it against the door jamb between the living room and the kitchen.

One night, Don got out of bed and started pacing around the house. "What's wrong?" "Nothing, go back to sleep." The same thing happened the next night, and the night after that.

"Don, please tell me what's wrong. Are you ok?"

"I can't sleep. I keep having a terrible nightmare."

"What is it?"

"I don't want to talk about it."

"Please tell me. Maybe I can help."

"OK. You asked for it. I see our daughter lying in a ditch and I know that I killed her."

"What? Why would you do that?"

"I don't know why. That's all there is. Then I wake up."

He was shaking as he told me, but he wasn't the only one frightened by his dream, and I talked him into seeing a counselor by promising to go with him. It only took two one-hour sessions for the doctor to declare that Don's dreams were his subconscious mind trying to rid him of the responsibility of being a father. He recommended Don continue private therapy sessions, but of course, he would not do that. The nightmares ended, or at least he never mentioned them again. Maybe talking about them and discovering why they were occurring was enough to make them stop.

CHAPTER NINE

In 1971, the year my third child was born, Gulf Oil transferred Dad to a city in western New York. It was a promotion for him and an opportunity he felt he couldn't pass up. Patty was married and living in Pennsylvania by then and Brandon was about to graduate from high school and did not want to make the move, choosing instead to stay in the area where he had grown up. So Dad went, leaving Mom and the others behind for a few months, allowing Brandon to finish up in school. She then went out to join him, along with the three youngest children. By then, Mom was having a great deal of trouble walking but still stubbornly refused to use a wheelchair. She often fell and got hurt, requiring a trip to the doctor or chiropractor.

With my family far away, I felt distanced from them and very much alone. By 1975, at the age of 28, I had become a single mother and the sole support of four children aged six months through nine. It was a difficult, sometimes miserable, sometimes scary time for me. But I knew my kids and I were all better off away from Don, even though the transition was hard on them too. Every year on Thanksgiving Eve I would pack everybody into my old station wagon and drive out to my parents' house for a visit. I know we stayed overnight, but for the life of me I cannot imagine where everyone slept. The visits were always fun and the dinner was always delicious. One year while I was there, one of my sisters got a phone call from the local blood bank. They were in urgent need of her rare blood type for a child who had been in a bad accident. I heard her on the phone. "Sure. And I'll bring my sister too. She has the same type blood." She hung up and looked at me. "Come on. We're going to give blood." "What?" I said. "I drive all the way out here for Thanksgiving and I end up going to see the vampires?" We were laughing as we walked out the door. And we came back with ugly coffee mugs that said, "I'm a blood donor," so it was definitely a worthwhile trip.

Back home, I worked hard and long; sometimes I had more than one job at a time. During a two-year stretch, I was classifying arrest fingerprints for a New York State agency on a night shift that lasted twelve-and-a-half hours a night, Friday, Saturday, and Sunday – the equivalent of a full week. Then, during the week I had a part time day job at a fast-food burger joint, and I managed to take a couple of college courses at night. Taking diet pills, 'uppers,' helped me function for those two years, but I got very little sleep and was sick most of the time, usually with bronchitis. I dealt with the constant stress of a long list of babysitters who made me late for work, stole things from my apartment, insisted on bringing their own kids or grandkids with them while they watched my children, or just quit without telling me they weren't going to show up any more. In the long run, the person who was the biggest help to me was my oldest child, my only daughter. She often cared for and cleaned up after her brothers, even though she was really just a child herself. But one thing I was absolutely sure of was that I would not quit working to raise my kids on welfare, I would not collect any kind of government handout. I believed that kids raised on welfare often lived the rest of their lives that way. I would not do that to them. More than anything, I loved my children. I did the best I could for them, but like my parents, I was poor and sometimes struggled to provide basic necessities. For many years we lived in a low-rent apartment complex, but the rooms were large and bright, we were in a good school district, and there were lots of other kids living there. There was little league, softball, basketball, scouting, and a great after-school program run by the town. And in the summer, we usually managed to spend a week tenting in Kennebunkport, Maine. We never had much, and I regret that I, like my dad, was never able to send any of my kids to college. But all in all, I think we did ok.

With only a high school diploma, I didn't have a lot of options open to me, but computers were in their infancy and there were not many people who were trained in computer science. I passed an aptitude test given by the state which was designed to identify people who could become good computer programmers, and my department took a chance on me. I was transferred to the day shift and moved upstairs for training. I learned to write code in two programming languages and embarked on a career that offered better money and more opportunity than I ever would have imagined. That changed my life.

***

In 1981, on the earliest date Dad was allowed to retire, he decided to bring Mom back home to the place where they had both grown up, where they still had family and he still had friends. They had been away for ten years. He didn't want to retire at 55, but Mom was becoming progressively more disabled and he felt compelled to stay home to take care of her. She could no longer walk or use her hands, but still she would call him names. She had once loved being the wife of a military officer. She had loved going to the Officers' Club on his arm and being seen with him when he was in uniform. It had made her feel special, important. She was always angry that he had taken that away from her to stay home and raise their children. When he said if he had remained in the military, he could well be six-feet-under with some of his friends, she called him 'spineless' and 'yellow-bellied.'

Dana was married and living in California, and the two youngest girls, who had finished high school and were working by then, were left behind. For the first time, my parents had no kids living with them. There was nobody in the house to give Dad a hand with even the simplest task or to pick up a loaf of bread or a carton of milk on the way home from somewhere. I was very busy with a full-time job and four growing children, but I did what I could to help Dad out. And when there was an occasion for Mom to give Dad a greeting card, such as Christmas or his birthday, I would shop for a card for her, take it to her so she could approve it, and sign it for her with "Love." Then I would always ask, "Shirley or Midge?" Midge had been Dad's name for my mother when they were first dating in high school. It was short for midget because he was very tall and she was very tiny. He didn't call her that any more, but he still addressed his cards to her that way. Her answer always depended on what kind of a mood she was in that day.

Working for Gulf Oil had never been his dream job, but this transition really knocked the wind out of his sails. He used to have daughters at home, go to work every day, be part of a bustling world and have stimulating conversations with interesting people. Now he was home alone, the full-time caregiver of his invalid wife. They bought a house two doors down from where Dad was raised. He quickly went to work redesigning the house to accommodate Mom's wheelchair. The only bathroom became part of the kitchen, with plenty of room for her to sit and watch as he cooked and did dishes. The two small bedrooms became a large bathroom where her needs could be taken care of. He built an addition on the back of the house which became a large bedroom, the only bedroom. It included two very large closets, one on either side of the room. In addition to accessing the bedroom from inside the house, he added an exterior door leading to the back deck so, in case of fire, he could get her quickly out of the bedroom, to the deck, to the ramp, to the back yard. Grandma was still living in Dad's childhood home and my father started walking over each morning just to check on her. It was he who found her the morning she did not wake up. Grandma's house had always felt so comfortable and warm to me as a child, but now she was gone and her house was bought by people we didn't know. They brought in carpenters and plumbers and masons and changed it all around, inside and out. Then they put a sign on the front yard that said, "APARTMENTS FOR RENT." It made me very sad.

Dad decided to take Mom on a cross-country trip to visit my sister in California. It had to be hard. With everything they needed packed and her wheelchair strapped to the floor of the van so she wouldn't roll, off they went. It was a long drive and they made a lot of overnight stops along the way. He had to get her out of the van and into the hotel, take care of her personal needs, feed her, lift her from the chair into bed and then start all over the next day. Dad had asked me to take care of his garden while they were gone. He was especially concerned about his blueberries. They had to be picked often, placed in the freezer on cookie sheets in a single layer so they wouldn't stick together and then, once frozen, put into plastic bags or containers. The cookie sheets took up a lot of room in the freezer, so I had to move some things around. Way in a back corner was a can of coffee. I grabbed it and something inside the can made a clunking sound. I opened the can and looked inside. What the hell?

For many years Mom had a half-moon conure, a small parrot about two inches longer than a parakeet. She called him Frenchie. The bird was often allowed to roam around the house and could be found sitting on the back of the sofa, perching on a curtain rod or walking across the dining room table. He liked being around people so we never had any trouble getting him to come to us if we wanted him to go back into his cage. He would sometimes swoop through the air and land on somebody's back, climbing up their shirt until he reached their shoulder where he would stay and beg for attention, rubbing his head against their neck. But he always preferred my mother and sometimes Mom's shoulder would be red and sore and full of scratches from the bird's sharp little claws. Mom never seemed to care; Frenchie was her friend when she sat for endless hours in her wheelchair. Now here was Frenchie, after a good long life, in a coffee can in my father's freezer. I knew he had died, but it never occurred to me that he hadn't been disposed of. I took the can out to the garden, dug a hole, and buried the bird, can and all.

My parents finally arrived at my sister's house and settled in for a nice visit. Dad looked forward to the California sunshine, some time with his daughter and her husband and, I'm sure, a little relief from being the only one in the house to cater to Mom's every need. There was a nice covered patio for Mom's wheelchair and even a heated pool, if he should feel like taking a dip. But several days before their intended departure my brother-in-law asked them to leave because he could not tolerate the unending lack of respect my mother showed to my father while they were there. At home, she often screwed up her face and stuck out her tongue at him to show she didn't care what he had to say. Or she would 'give him the raspberry', or spit. Apparently, she could not manage to act civilly even in someone else's home. I can only imagine how that made Dad feel. My sister was the one who told me about it; Dad never said a word.

When they arrived back home, Dad needed something to do. He had always loved trains, so in the basement, even though it was one of those old basements where he could not stand up straight without hitting his head, he busied himself constructing an amazing miniature village. He used chicken wire, plaster, paper mâché and paint. He created hills and trees and streams. His village had houses, a market, retail stores, a bank, a post office, churches, and schools. It had bridges and tunnels. There were cars and trucks and people, some walking, some on bikes – tiny little figures that he ordered from a catalogue. And of course, there were trains. Three of them, all crisscrossing each other on their way to wherever they were going. Every time I thought it was finished, he came up with something else he wanted to add. It was really quite impressive, but never really done. At Christmastime, the youth group from our church would always go out caroling, visiting the ill and the injured. Dad's house was on the list of destinations every year because of Mom, and Dad always rewarded them with hot chocolate for all and a trip to the basement, so everyone could take a turn running his trains.

CHAPTER TEN

As Mom's condition worsened to the point where they could no longer carry on a conversation, Dad became very lonely. No matter how often I tried to go down there, it was never enough. I was still working and lived forty-five minutes away from him so he didn't complain, but he would greet me with, "Hello, Stranger," when I walked in. It was his way of telling me he wanted to see me more often. I was able to convince him, after much resistance, to learn how to use a computer so he could stay in touch with his kids via email. It was all very foreign to him at first and he would call me constantly, often while I was at work, asking for guidance. He called me his 'computer expert.' He wrote lots of notes in a steno notepad to help himself remember the things I taught him, and besides sending and receiving emails, he discovered he enjoyed playing solitaire on his computer. He also spent a lot of time sifting through old family photos, sorting them, labeling them. Many went back to his grandparents and great-grandparents, his aunts and uncles and cousins. Mom's family too. We would often look at them together while he identified for me as many people as he could. Because of those hours spent with him I now have several albums to enjoy and pass on. There are pictures of my grandparents as children, pictures of my parents in high school, pictures of family picnics and gatherings, pictures of Dad in uniform, standing next to a Quonset hut or a military plane. They are all really fun to look at, and I am glad to have them.

After all those years of struggling to support his family, he now had pensions from both Gulf Oil and the Air Force. He and Mom finally had money to spend on their retirement, money to travel, to do fun things. But she had become completely disabled and there would be no fun. Dad started writing checks to every quack organization that sent him junk mail. The more his name got shared, the more requests he got. I had no idea he was throwing his money away like that. One day he said to me, "Carol, they keep asking me for more money even though I just sent them a check. I don't know what to do." I said, "Dad, they keep asking you for more money because you keep sending it! Just stop." And political campaigns. It didn't matter who it was, or what their platform was. If they sent a request for a donation, he complied. Some politicians would include photos of themselves and he started framing them and putting them up in his house as if they were his friends. He wasn't losing his marbles; he just felt lonely and isolated and, except for turning the pages in Mom's book hour after hour so she could read, useless.

By now Dad had lost his faith. I don't know exactly when it happened. I expect it was a slow, gradual realization that he really didn't believe all those stories he'd been fed as a child, just as it was for me. We never talked about it. I had come to the conclusion, completely on my own and with much guilt and trepidation, that religion, no matter which one, was created partly to control the masses, partly for financial gain, and partly because we humans cannot face things like guilt, suffering, inequity or death without the crutch of religion to buoy us up. I still love the Christmas story, but for me now it is just a beautiful story, a fairy tale. I was sorry for him that he let go of it, because believing that you will someday again see a lost loved one is much more comforting than understanding that death is final and there will be no miraculous reunions in the sky.

He tried to stay busy with his trains, his accordion, and a small garden. Dad had often experimented with his own version of organic gardening and we never knew when we'd find something strange in the garden or hanging from his fruit trees. One example that stands out for me was the day he proudly took me out back to show me a dozen or so small plastic containers suspended from strings in the branches of his peach trees. They had some awful-smelling concoction in them that was supposed to attract and kill bugs. I don't know if it worked, but the trees sure looked comical. If someone else had done it, he'd have used one of his favorite words and called it a 'cockamamie' idea. He caught rainwater in a big barrel for watering the garden and he collected kitchen scraps for composting. But he was deflated; he didn't have much of a life. Mom lived her last twenty-five years in a wheel chair, cared for by the man who had loved her since they were teenagers. She could not use her arms or legs, hold her head up, feed herself, use the bathroom – but she could still spit. Sometimes as he leaned down to try to understand what she was saying, if her mind was in an angry place, even though he was the person who took care of her, loved her every single day, she would spit at him. And he would say nothing.

Mom was completely dependent upon Dad but still he allowed her to call most of the shots. With an invalid wife at home he almost never went anywhere or did any of the things he enjoyed. He loved German music and German beer, but when he wanted to take her to a local Octoberfest for a few hours, she refused. I offered to stay with her so he could go but that made her mad so he stayed home. It was the same if friends asked them over. Hopefully, with a smile on his face, he would ask her if she'd like to go visit so-and-so for a little while. He tried to make it sound like fun, like trying to convince a child to do something. She would say no; they would stay home. When members of the church got together to work on the Pastor's house, she threw a fit because he wanted to go and help. They were his friends; he wanted to participate. But once again she won out. It used to make me so mad! I told him to just go and I would stay with her, but he wouldn't do it. I once got a phone call at work from our family doctor. He said Dad was there, he had the flu and he was too sick and weak to drive home. Doc asked if I would come and get him. I did. I took him home, called my brother to go get his car, gave him some tea and soup and crackers and put him to bed. Then I went into the living room to sit with Mom. That wasn't good enough for her. She wanted him. I explained that he was sick and needed to get some rest. Still not good enough. She couldn't really speak much, but she yelled, "Bill!" Mind you, it wasn't that she was worried about him. She was just demanding his attention. I said, "Mom, Dad needs to get some sleep." "BIIIIILLLLLLLL!!!!!" It was clear she didn't care what he needed. So, I put my face very close to hers and said quietly but with anger in my voice, "Mom, if Dad doesn't get some rest, he'll get even sicker and he'll have to go to the hospital. Then what are you going to do?" She shut up.

I cannot describe the terrible guilt that comes with hating your own mother, especially when she becomes so devastatingly incapacitated. For nearly my entire life I had dealt with her anger, her jealousy, her spitefulness, her downright nasty disposition. She had often made me feel infuriated,

132

miserable, and resentful. Now she was so incredibly broken and I felt sorry for her. I felt sorry for Dad. I felt sorry for me.

Mom got weaker and slept a lot, often in her wheelchair. She choked when she tried to swallow, so she didn't want to drink, and several times she had to go to the hospital to be treated for severe dehydration. By the time she made her final trip to the hospital, it had become obvious that chances were good she would never go home again. In a nearly imperceptible voice, she said to Dad, "I'm dying." He responded, "I'm afraid you may be right, Dear." A doctor suggested a feeding tube. Usually no one but my father could any longer understand her, but when she looked at the doctor and said, "Go to hell!" the doctor responded, "Well, that was clear!" Despite that, Dad ignored her wishes and approved the feeding tube. He was desperate. He didn't want her to die. When I said I understood how he felt, but it should be her decision, he said, "Not really. She's my wife." I said, "Dad, Mom has lived like this a long, long time and she doesn't want to do it anymore. Her life isn't good, no matter how hard you try." He choked back a sob and I felt terrible, but it had to be said. Still, the next day she had a feeding tube. But her body rejected any nutrition they tried to put through it, so it ended up being used only to administer medications.

One day I got to spend a little time alone with Mom. She was being moved to hospice and I needed to talk to her. For both of us. "I love you" were words that were never said in our house when I was growing up. I don't believe I ever heard that phrase spoken. Saying it was too intimate, too uncomfortable. It was like saying "pregnant." You couldn't, you had to say "expecting." "Pregnant" made people squirm. It was different for my kids. I had said "I love you" to them since they were born and it seemed easy and natural for them to say it back. But not my parents. I sat down by Mom and looked in her eyes. I said, "I love you Mom." She stared at me. I wasn't sure she'd understood so I said it again. "Mom, I said I love you." In a labored, barely audible, broken whisper she asked, "You love me?" I said, "Yes. You're my mother and I love you. I'm sorry you have this terrible disease and I'm sorry your life has been so hard. You got cheated. Dad got cheated. We all got cheated." By now most of my family had come in from their various corners of the country and Mom had seen each one as they arrived. I sat with her a little while and then she tried to say something to me. It was two syllables. She said it over and over. Each time, try as I might, I'd have to respond with, "Mom, I'm sorry, I can't understand what you're saying." It was clearly important to her because she kept trying. It sounded the same each time: "ail...um" "ail...um," with a long, strained pause between the two syllables. I felt so bad. I think now if I'd asked her if she could spell it for me, just the first letter would have been all I needed. But it wasn't until several nights after she was gone that, as I lay awake repeating it over and over again in my head, I suddenly realized what she'd been saying. She hadn't had the strength to pronounce the two beginning consonants. She was trying to ask if the last of her children was coming. "Dale come." My sister Dale was not there and Mom was waiting for her. Dale was not coming.

CHAPTER ELEVEN

Dad made another decision during this time that surprised most of us, and the way he told us is an example of how there can be humor even in a sad situation. My youngest sister is a nurse, so he directed his comment to her. "Denise," he said solemnly, "I've decided to donate your mother's head for research." My sister could not stifle a chuckle. "No Dad, not her head. You mean you've decided to donate her brain." Arrangements were made with a research hospital in New York City, and after Mom passed, the procedure was immediately executed and the donation was made.

When she died at the age of 73, he was lost. They had been married for fifty-four years. He was one month shy of his seventy-fifth birthday, strong, healthy. We all hoped he would rally and finally have some fun. Travel. Learn a new hobby. But that was not in the cards. "Do you know what your mother said to me just before she died?" he asked. "She said 'I love you.'" To him it was a momentous thing and I could tell it made him incredibly happy. I believe I taught her how to say it a few days before, when I had said the same to her. In stark contrast, as we were all gathered at Dad's house a few days after Mom's passing, one of my sisters could not contain herself and shouted, "I'm glad she's dead! I hated her and she hated me!"

Some of us went with Dad to plan Mom's service. He chose her favorite hymns and picked out a recent picture of the two of them to set on a table in the foyer of the church, just outside the sanctuary, where people would see it as they entered. In the photo, Mom was hunched over in her wheelchair, straining to raise her head just enough to look at the camera. There was a faint, crooked smile on her lips, but her eyes showed the many hard years of her illness. Dad was kneeling alongside her wheelchair, his hand on her shoulder. I asked, "Dad, can we use two pictures?" "Well, I don't see why not," he replied. "Which one do you have in mind?" "This one," I said, pulling out the photo that had been taken of them on their wedding day. He grinned at me. "OK."

11/16/1946

Many people filled the church that day. At that time, I was a member of a local a cappella chorus, a chapter of Sweet Adelines, and a number of my singing friends were there. I sat in the front of the familiar church with the rest of my family, and some of us took turns saying something about Mom. When it was my turn, I talked about how much Mom had loved birds and that I believed they signified for her the freedom she had lost to her illness so many years ago. Then I began to sing the old hymn "I'll Fly Away." Unexpectedly, without any prompting, some of my friends began to join in from the back of the church, then more and more until the sanctuary was filled with four-part harmony. The pastor told me later, "I've never experienced anything so spontaneous and uplifting." It was an incredible moment, because of music, and the love and support of my friends.

In an attempt to begin socializing again, Dad occasionally went to a Senior Citizens pot luck dinner at a local church and he often told me about the other people who had been there. He'd known many of them for most of his life and he sometimes made me laugh with the comments he made. He once said the 'old biddies' couldn't wait to see what he had brought because he could cook circles around all of them, but he said it with a twinkle in his eye and I knew he was teasing. When I suggested he might think of someone he could take out to dinner or a movie he said, "Your mother is still in my heart." I replied that I didn't expect him to have a big romance, but he could still make a friend, enjoy somebody's company. He didn't object, but it never happened. I decided to take him to California to see my sister. We flew out together and it was odd to see how confused Dad was by the process of switching planes. "How do we know what gate to go to and how do we know where it is? What if we can't find it? What if we miss our plane?" He hadn't flown in a very long time. The day after we arrived, the three of us were standing in my sister's pool, talking and enjoying the sunshine. Dad said he'd recently watched a medical program on public television and they talked about feeding tubes in graphic detail. "I'm so sorry I did that to your mother," he said. I assured him that he'd done what he thought was right at the time, and that seemed to ease his mind. Later, Dana and I started to reminisce about our childhood. We were remembering all kinds of things, a few of which Dad never knew. When we brought up some of the hurtful things Mom had done, he looked at us incredulously and said, "MY wife?" Dana and I glanced at each other and I responded, "Dad, what house were you living in when we were growing up? It couldn't have been the same house we were in."

In my opinion, his best quality was perhaps his only weakness, the thing that often drove me nuts when I was growing up, and one way in which I am definitely not like him. That was his ability to not get angry even when he was being treated badly, to not see bad things in people even when sometimes there really were bad things to see, to "just let things slide," as he used to say. I have a lot of patience and I can take a lot of crap, but push me too far and I fight back. Dad was a great example of looking at the world through rose-colored glasses. Sometimes you have to take the glasses off. Did he really love her so much that he was completely oblivious to the terrible way she treated people, the terrible way she treated him? Or was it just that he'd invested so much in their marriage, his entire life, in fact, that he could not bear to see how very sad the whole thing was? I didn't understand it then and I don't understand it now. I'm pretty sure I never will.

He had many pictures from his time in the military and he remembered most of the guys in them. Many of them exchanged Christmas cards over the years, so he had addresses, too. He chose a date, mailed out hand-written invitations and managed to convince a small group of men to come to his house for a reunion. They had all met when they were overseas and they came from all over the country. He asked me to play hostess, so I spent the afternoon serving snacks and drinks while they all sat around his dining room table reminiscing. The stories I heard! One of them had been a pilot and had to abandon his plane over the ocean. He said he had only two thoughts as he parachuted into the water: "I hope I don't die today," and "I'm gonna have a lot of explaining to do." They had all been so young and had done such amazing things. But when they started sharing what colleges they had attended on the GI bill, what degrees they had gotten, what jobs they'd had, what wonderful trips they'd been able to take and how successful their children had become, I could see the sadness in Dad's face. Regret, disappointment. He had done none of those things. And he hadn't been able to send any of his kids to college. He had worked hard all his life. He'd been a fine upstanding citizen, a good, respectful, thoughtful, well-liked, honest, reliable man. He'd been active in church and in the community. He'd been a good son, a good father, a good husband. But he had not come close to reaching his potential. He had not met any of his lofty-but-attainable goals. He had always done the right thing – for everyone but himself. At dinnertime we all went to a small local restaurant. Dad had already pre-ordered everyone's meal – his favorite item on the menu. That amused me; it was so like Dad. It never occurred to him that someone might want something different. He just made a decision and took care of it. There were more stories. More laughter. Old men remembering the incredible responsibility that had been placed on their shoulders by the military at such a very young age. I will never forget that day.

Dad began to decline both physically and mentally. How could this be happening? He was only in his mid-70s and had been so healthy. He began to fall. My big, strong dad would just topple over, bewildered that his legs had given out. One day I took him out to lunch and as we were walking across the windy parking lot his cap blew off. It was rolling across the blacktop and he instinctively ran to grab it before it got away, but after only two steps he crashed to the ground. He hit his face on the pavement and when he looked up his mouth was all bloody. A security officer saw what had happened and ran over to help him up. He had a dental bridge and the metal had pierced the inside of his mouth and was not letting go. I wanted to take him to the hospital but he said no, he was fine. I drove him home and called his dentist. They had to cut the inside of his cheek, remove the bridge and build him a new one. When I asked, "Why in the world did you run after that baseball cap?" he said one of his grandsons had given it to him and he didn't want to lose it.

The mind that could process numbers like a computer could no longer figure out how to build a simple bookshelf. He gave up and tossed his hammer across the room. Every house he and Mom had owned over the years had felt the blow of his hammer. He'd moved walls, installed cabinets and counter tops and sinks, built decks and additions, replaced windows and doors. You name it, he could do it. Plumbing? Wiring? No problem. He'd figure it out. It may not have been a professional job, but it always worked. So, the day I walked into his house and found him frustrated and confused over how to assemble that small shelf, the scene tugged at my heartstrings. I could have helped him, but that would have made him feel worse. Without comment I picked up the hammer, the nails, and the wood and put them away.

He still kept a little bucket on the kitchen counter for food scraps intended for his compost heap. In the past he'd been good about taking it out on a regular basis, but lately he was either forgetting or just couldn't physically make the trip outside. Every time I went to his house, the first thing I noticed when I walked into his kitchen was the smell of garbage. I said, "Dad, no more composting. It's too much for you to take care of. I'm getting rid of this little bucket." He thought for a short moment, gave me a look of resignation and replied, "OK, Boss."

He'd always been tall and thin, but he was losing an alarming amount of weight and didn't want to eat. He would say "nothing tastes good." I would prepare individual meals for him and put them in the freezer so he could just pop them in the microwave. Uncle Jim, who lived closer to him than I, checked on him often. My uncle would find meals I had made, sitting on the counter, thawed, uncooked, spoiled. A couple of times he said, "Carol, your father can't live alone anymore." But Dad was stubborn. He didn't want to leave his home and I knew if I brought it up, he would just dig in his heels. During his illness, I had retired from my job. I was able to go down more often and take him to his doctor appointments, which by now had become very frequent. It seemed that they tested every organ in his body and could find nothing wrong. At one point I thought his symptoms mimicked some of the things I'd seen in my mother when she had MS. I asked his doctor if it was possible that he missed her so much he was showing psychosomatic symptoms of her illness. She said no. I still naively believed that once they did the right test and found out what was making him sick, they would treat him and make him whole again. I believe he thought so too.

I decided to take him to the emergency room after walking into his house and finding him slumped over on the couch, barely able to lift his head. I was in the exam room with him when a neurologist came in with a student. He began to examine Dad, talking to the student the whole time. At first, he said it looked like MS. Really? Had I been right when I asked his doctor if his symptoms could be psychosomatic? Was Dad so brokenhearted that he was making himself sick? It seemed impossible to me that both my parents could actually be stricken with the same disease. Then the doctor asked Dad to stick out his tongue. He looked at his student and said no, it was not MS. Because of the way the sides of Dad's tongue curled up, it looked more like ALS. When he said that, I couldn't believe my ears. I told him Dad's younger brother had died from ALS. It couldn't possibly run in families, could it? Well, yes. A small percentage of ALS is genetic. It is called familial ALS. A test would be needed to confirm the diagnosis. Dad was admitted to the hospital and wheeled upstairs. When the test results came back positive, the doctor said he thought it would be best if I were to tell him. I asked the doctor, "Does he have to know?" The doctor said if I didn't want to tell him, he would. I sat on Dad's hospital bed, put my arms around his neck, leaned in and whispered, "Dad, I'm so sorry. You have ALS." Nothing. I whispered again. Again nothing. I leaned back, looked in his eyes and said, "Dad, did you hear what I said?" He yelled, "Yes I heard you! I have what my brother had. What do you want me to do – cry about it?" The man who almost never showed anger was dying and he knew it and he was railing against the reality. He had watched his brother waste away at the age of sixty-five. He knew what was coming. He felt lost and scared, and so did I. I hugged him and started to cry. I said, "I'm so sorry Dad. This is hard for me too. I hate that this is happening to you." He was only seventy-seven, and he had spent all those years caring for my mother. It just wasn't fair.

The next day my brother and I asked him to sign a Power of Attorney so we could pay his bills and take care of whatever else needed to be done. He thought about it for a minute and then with his jaw clenched and fire in his eyes he signed the paper. Then he signed his arm. Then he signed the bedsheet. When he reached toward the wall with his pen, I took his hand in mine and said quietly, "Dad, you can stop now." That was probably the only temper tantrum he'd had in his entire life, and a few days later he was dead.

During his short stay there, my youngest sister, the nurse, had asked permission from the hospital staff to bathe him. She wanted to be the one to take care of him, but I knew it was going to be very emotional for her, so I told her I would stay with her. We pulled the curtain around his hospital bed and she slowly uncovered and disrobed him. He was so incredibly emaciated. His ribs stuck out and his hip bones nearly poked through his skin. I bit my lip and held back my tears as Denise did what nurses do all the time. But this time it was different. This time it was Dad. She was amazing.

Brandon and I lived close by, but Patty had come from Pennsylvania and Dana from California. Denise was also there. Our remaining sister had given birth to a baby boy two days earlier and was not able to come. My brother and I happened to be in the room, standing at the foot of his bed talking with his doctor, when we heard him gasp. We all looked up and stared at him. His chest stopped moving. The doctor called for a nurse, grabbed her stethoscope, listened for a heartbeat, looked at the clock on the wall and pronounced the time of death. Just like that. It was over. Brandon and I hugged each other and cried. Through his tears he asked me, "How are we gonna do it without Dad?" I had no answer for him. At the neurologist's suggestion, Dad's DNA was sent to Northwestern University. It didn't mean much at the time, because after two years of waiting I was told the gene that had caused his ALS (and presumably his brother's) was not yet understood well enough to test family members. Years went by and my sister Patty developed the disease. I got back in touch with the University and found out that the gene had been researched and identified as C9ORF72 in 2011 and now there was a test.

On March 3, 2016 it claimed Patty. A few months before, I had gone for a visit and we spent several wonderful days together. We played board games and Canasta. One of her hands no longer worked at all and she could barely use the other one, so we had to rig up a way for her to hold her cards, but she could still beat me. When we tired of that she taught me a new game called 'Sequence.' We watched old movies and reminisced. Shortly after I got home, she sent me a note. "Carol, you're good at this stuff. I want you to do something for me. I want you to make arrangements to donate my brain for research." Oh, Patty! I crumbled into a sobbing, heartbroken puddle. But this was important; I had to do it for my sister, and for her kids. I emailed my contact at Northwestern University and asked some questions. I was told they would gladly accept her offer, but it would be most helpful to them if they could also receive her spinal cord. I relayed the message to Patty and she said yes. From there, I put Patty's husband in touch with the University and passed the torch to him. Now their four children are at risk and everyone worries, waiting to see who will be next. Maybe my sister's extraordinary gift will help find a cure.

CHAPTER TWELVE

It is 2018 and the popularity of DNA testing for the purpose of building family trees is exploding. I've been poking around on ancestry.com for quite some time and have become very good at doing research on their site, creating a fairly large tree for my family as well as one for my husband's family. I had submitted my sample a while ago and one of my sisters had too. When she came back as my first cousin, I thought it was amusing, not yet realizing the accuracy of all this, and blew it off. I completely ignored the strange result, actually even forgetting about it for quite a while. Then I learned about a piece of information that resides on the website that I had not previously discovered. Curious, I looked again at my match with my sister. The centimorgan count said we were half siblings. The 'first cousin' designation was really just about degrees of separation and, for me, very misleading. I looked at our common matches. I had four cousins that she did not. I started researching those four names, found that somewhere in their families they all had a common last name, and was then able to trace them back to the common ancestor. I am 71-years-old and just found out that my dad, the man I loved and looked up to and depended on and learned from my whole life, was not my father.

So, what do you do when you discover something about yourself that is so shocking, so completely unexpected, that it rattles you to your very core? You cry. You chew, swallow, and digest the information. Then you wait, think, and cry some more. For two weeks I walked around in a bit of a stupor. I was sure Dad never knew. I couldn't sleep; I started writing. Everything I could remember just came pouring out of me. Dad once said to me, "Carol, your mother told me that I was never around when you were little and you kids won't remember me when I'm gone. Will you remember me?" Oh yes, Dad, look. Look at all the things I'm writing about. I wish you could read this now. I wish I could tell you now. But you can't hear me anymore.

I had the name, unfamiliar to me, of the man I believed fathered me. By contacting some other matches on the ancestry website, I was able to get in touch with one of this man's daughters. She is older than me and she was very accepting; she did not push me away or shut me down. In fact, she sent in her DNA sample so I could have confirmation. The result was not a surprise; she is one of my new half-sisters. I have since met her and hope to spend more time with her. I like her very much.

When I told them about my revelation, two more of the sisters I grew up with ordered their testing kits. As expected, they are also my half-siblings.

Ironically, I'm the only one who has been tested to see if I inherited the ALS gene. I decided to have the test done as soon as I learned it was available so I could tell my kids whether or not I may have passed it down to any of them. I was very relieved to get back a negative result. Now I know the reason I didn't inherit the gene. I don't have any of Dad's genes. I didn't need to get tested.

I drove to the home of my dad's brother and his wife, my Uncle Jim and Aunt Gina. Despite their advanced ages, they're still pretty sharp. I was afraid of how they would react when I told them Dad was not my biological father. Would they believe me? Would they believe DNA evidence? Would they be shocked, angry, sad? Or would they just laugh it off? But my news didn't surprise them at all. Looking me right in the eye, they sent a shockwave through me when they both admitted that my dad's entire family, including my grandma, knew from the day I was born that I was not his child. I just sat there dumbfounded, staring across the table at them, my hand covering my gaping mouth. "Dad knew?!" "Yes, Carol." "Oh my god….."

***

The day he arrived home on leave in 1946, he was greeted by a fiancée who was desperate to get married. He didn't understand the urgency she felt. He knew she missed him when he was away and he missed her too, but they had their whole lives ahead of them and he was enjoying his life in the military. He wasn't ready to tie the knot. Whether she finally told him or he simply figured it out, somehow during this time he became aware of her condition. Still, despite that, and despite his hesitation, my mother wore him down. How? What could she possibly have said to him? My uncle said, "Bill took our mother into the bedroom and shut the door, but I could hear them. He said, 'Ma, Shirley's expecting, and it can't possibly be my baby.' I knew I shouldn't eavesdrop, so I left the room and didn't hear the rest of their conversation." My grandmother was a kind, God-fearing woman and I can only imagine the advice she must have given him.

Dad knew the first time he held me that some other man had fathered me, but he loved me anyhow and never treated me one ounce differently than my five younger siblings. I never had even the tiniest doubt that he was my father. Ever. With this revelation from my aunt and uncle, I was all at once heartbroken, grateful and a little lost. My uncle said, "Carol, he stepped up to the plate and did what was right." That was my dad. He always stepped up to the plate.

I know my biological father's name. He was twelve years older than my mother and they both worked for the same small heating oil company when Mom first got out of high school. But he was not my dad. My dad was the man who gave up a potentially limitless career in the U.S. Air Force to give me and my mother a safe and secure life, even though he knew my young mother, his high school sweetheart, was carrying someone else's child. He's the man who loved me from the day I was born until the day I watched him die. Love is not made of DNA.

***

Thinking back, Dad gave me two hints during his lifetime. The first one, I'm sure, was inadvertent. I was a teenager, sometimes sweet, sometimes bratty – or worse. I had walked to a friend's house, angry about something, and after I refused to come home he came over to get me. As we walked silently side by side toward home, he blurted out, "You know, you ruined my life." I didn't respond. I didn't ask what he meant. I was too busy feeling indignant. I just thought he was mad at me. But for some reason those words always stuck in my mind. Maybe because it was so unlike Dad to say something hurtful. He never said anything like that to me again. Oh, how I wish I knew what he was thinking when he uttered those words. If only I had asked him.

The second hint was when I was long into adulthood, with a career and living on my own with four children. He had decided to write a memoir of his military service and had been working on it for quite a while. He then asked me if I would proofread it, make corrections and type it up for him so it could be put into a binder. He talked about his navigation and radar training. He talked about APQ-7 radar and the B-29 he flew in, once going to 42,000 feet, much higher than normal operating altitude. He talked about Guam, Honolulu, Okinawa, Kwajalein Atoll and Tinian. And he relayed this story: "On one flight to Guam, we had arrived late and planned to stay overnight. We were at the Officers' Club having a drink when a Colonel came over to us and asked for Lt. Williams. Our pilot talked to him and was told that we would have a passenger going back to Okinawa. Overnight our B-29 had been moved from the far end of the runway up to a point in front of Operations. In the cockpit window was a red plaque with four gold stars. Our passenger was General Jimmy Doolittle. During the flight, he sat on the front nosewheel hatch right behind the pilots. He was very informal and we kidded a lot with him. Right at that time the Armed Forces had a point system to determine the order in which men were returned from overseas. My recollection is that 27 was the magic number. This was based on number of months overseas, battle stars, etc. We laughingly asked the General how many points he had. To my best recollection, it was close to 100. He signed my 'short snorter.' This was an Air Force custom whereby paper money from each place the individual visited was taped together. Then the object was to get the signature of everyone that we encountered." What Dad didn't write down, but explained to me, was that when servicemen gathered at a bar, the man with the shortest string of bills had to buy a 'snort' for everyone there. Thus, the name 'short snorter.' Dad's is six bills long. The signatures are a bit faded, but with a magnifying glass you can read "James Doolittle." I had it framed in UV-protective glass and it hangs on my wall.

After reading his hand-written draft I did fix a few minor things, but Dad was a good writer. Mostly I was just an extra pair of eyes. I moved a few sentences around but never changed the content. I never checked or questioned any of the dates – those were in his head, not mine, and I assumed they were correct. But he was telling me right there! He could not have been my father. I was proof-reading it, typing it and not seeing it. Did he do this on purpose? Had he given me a puzzle to figure out because he couldn't bring himself to tell me? I love puzzles, I'm great at solving them. But this one slipped right by me. Dad was very busy, in another part of the world, when I was conceived.

***

After my discussion with my dad's brother I talked to Aunt Lana who said she always thought it was wrong that nobody had ever told me. Then she told me something else. At first, she said, Dad accused Uncle Jim because he had spent a lot of time with Mom, taking her wherever he happened to be going – often at Grandma's insistence – so she wouldn't always be alone while Dad was away. That got straightened out and then Aunt Lana's husband (Dad's brother Kyle) had told her that my 'real' father was my maternal grandfather – Grumpy! What?! "Yes, Carol, your grandfather was a terrible drinker, and nasty when he was drunk. He went home one night and raped his daughter – your mother." WHAT?! Was that an assumption that was made, based on Grumpy's love of booze and his reputation for being abusive to my grandmother? Possible. Or could it have been a story Mom made up so Dad would feel sorry for her and marry her? Entirely possible. I can't imagine her ever saying, "Bill, I'm so sorry. While you were away serving our country, I was fooling around with J. Z. at work, but please marry me anyhow."

Or, did Mom's father actually rape her? Also entirely possible, I suppose. If he did, who did Mom think was my father – J. Z. or her own father? Was she tortured by the uncertainty? Did she tell J. Z., who was married, about me? Was she terrified of her future? I shudder to think what might have happened to her, what might have happened to me. And if Mom was in fact raped by her own father, did HE think I was his child? Does that explain him telling my cousin I could get away with things that she couldn't because I was 'his favorite?' Of course, because of DNA testing I know without a doubt who my biological father was, but what in the world did they all think? It's a question that haunts me, but one I'll never be able to answer.

After she died and before I knew all this, I tried so hard to understand and forgive my mother. I was actually making progress. I had many one-sided 'conversations' with her, hoping for some insight into why she was the way she was. Neither she nor my father drank, except for an occasional beer or glass of wine, and there was no drug abuse. Maybe she'd been traumatized somehow. Maybe she was mentally ill; I often thought she might be. Whatever the reason, I was beginning to believe she did not choose to be the way she was. Nobody makes a conscious decision to be miserable.

But now I have new information to factor in. She was young, pregnant out of wedlock during a time when that would have been a disgrace, and living in a very small rural town where she could not have escaped the humiliation should the truth be known. So, was Mom nasty to Dad's family because they knew her secret and she couldn't stand the guilt? Is that why she so desperately wanted Dad to stay in the military instead of moving back home to all the whispers? Was she afraid her own family would find out? As far as I can tell after talking to those that are left, no one on Mom's side ever spoke about any suspicions they must have had. Her sister seemed genuinely surprised when I told her.

Was Mom afraid I would find out? And if she made up that story about her father raping her so Dad wouldn't leave her, was she afraid either my dad or her father (or both) would find out that she had told a terrible lie? Did that explain her complete meltdown on the kitchen floor when she heard my grandfather had died? Or did that uncontrollable release of emotions happen because he really had raped her and she had lived all those years not being able to confront him? And even if this awful secret caused her to be paranoid and nasty and suspicious and mean to others, it doesn't excuse the way she treated Dad. He was the one who was on her side, the one who married her and protected her and raised her daughter as his own. Why did she belittle him, call him names? Why did she try to diminish him in the eyes of his children? Why did she spit at him when she could no longer do anything else? And why did she sometimes take pleasure in hurting her own children? Even if she somehow held me responsible for her dilemma, the other kids certainly had no part in it. Mom wanted so badly for me to be smarter, more talented, more competent than my paternal cousins. Was that because she felt the need to justify my existence to Dad's family, to prove that the mistake she had made wasn't so bad after all?

I am so grateful for the father I grew up with, for his example, for his council, for his steadfastness, for the precious gift of his love and his time. I can't help but wonder if or when or how often he may have looked at me and thought about the fact that I was some other man's child. But then I remind myself that I am his daughter, I was always his daughter because he chose to make me his daughter. I am grateful beyond belief that he loved my mother and me enough to sacrifice his dreams and settle for a life that was not what he wanted, not what he clearly deserved. And I am grateful for his mother, my grandma, who taught him to be the man he was.

Dad, I so wish you were here. I desperately need to hug you.

Author's Note

The memories described in this book are solely mine, based on my best recollections. I recognize and acknowledge that many years have gone by and others may remember some details differently.

Carol Caloro lives with her husband of twelve years, in a small town in upstate New York, less than an hour's drive from where she grew up. This is her first book.

CPSIA information can be obtained
at www.ICGtesting.com
Printed in the USA
FFHW021347300419
52080846-57529FF

9 781644 385661